GARDEN BUILDER

Plans and Instructions *for* 35 Projects You Can Make

JOANN MOSER

COOL
SPRINGS
PRESS

Brimming with creative inspiration, how-to projects, and useful information to enrich your everyday life, Quarto Knows is a favorite destination for those pursuing their interests and passions. Visit our site and dig deeper with our books into your area of interest: Quarto Creates, Quarto Cooks, Quarto Homes, Quarto Lives, Quarto Drives, Quarto Explores, Quarto Gifts, or Quarto Kids.

First published in 2018 by Cool Springs Press, an imprint of The Quarto Group, 401 Second Avenue North, Suite 310, Minneapolis, MN 55401 USA.
T (612) 344-8100 F (612) 344-8692
www.QuartoKnows.com

Cool Springs Press titles are also available at discount for retail, wholesale, promotional, and bulk purchase. For details, contact the Special Sales Manager by email at specialsales@quarto.com or by mail at The Quarto Group, Attn: Special Sales Manager, 401 Second Avenue North, Suite 310, Minneapolis, MN 55401 USA.

10 9 8 7 6 5 4 3 2 1

ISBN: 978-0-7603-5393-6

Library of Congress Cataloging-in-Publication Data

Names: Moser, JoAnn, 1963- author.
Title: Garden builder : complete plans for creative outdoor projects you can build / JoAnn Moser.
Description: Minneapolis, Minnesota : Cool Springs Press, [2018] | Includes bibliographical references and index.
Identifiers: LCCN 2017041349 | ISBN 9780760353936 (pb)
Subjects: LCSH: Garden ornaments and furniture--Design and construction
Classification: LCC SB473.5 .M68 2018 | DDC 684.1/8--dc23
LC record available at https://lccn.loc.gov/2017041349

Acquiring Editor: Mark Johanson
Editor: Bryan Trandem
Project Manager: Jordan Wiklund
Art Director: Brad Springer
Cover Designer: Lauren Vajda
Project Construction by Nick Moser
Layout: Lauren Vajda
Illustrations: Christopher Mills

Printed in China

Acknowledgments

SPECIAL THANKS TO Mark Johanson for the opportunity to work, once again, with him and his stellar team at Cool Springs Press, including (but not limited to) Brad Springer and Jordan Wiklund. From copy editing to book layout and design and everything in between, they are the magicians that turned my words and photographs into an honest-to-goodness book. Thanks, also, to Alisa Carbone for her help in spreading the word.

Another person whose contribution directly influenced the existence of *Garden Builder* is my DIY cohort Nick Moser. The strong hands in the forthcoming pages are his, as he constructed the vast majority of the projects you're about to see. We always design as a team, but his is the voice of reason when rules of mechanics are involved. In that way, he supplies the much-needed substance to my style. Although I lobbied to have Nick's name included on the cover of this book right next to mine, he demurred, perfectly content to be my silent—but fiercest—champion. Thank you, my love.

Contents

Introduction

HAVE YOU EVER WANTED TO ADD PERSONALITY TO YOUR GARDEN? Or needed a utilitarian item to make your gardening experience more enjoyable? Have you gone to a garden center or big box store but couldn't find exactly what you were looking for—or maybe you could find it but you couldn't afford it?

I can't tell you how many times this has happened to me. I'm lucky to live with a woodworker who owns just about every woodworking tool imaginable. If I can't find what I want at the store, or it's too expensive, I can sketch up a design and place an order with my very own handy-person.

Not everyone is as lucky as I am. And that's where the projects in *Garden Builder* come into play. Chosen for their ease of construction, the woodworking projects utilize simple joinery and can be made with common hand tools such as a drills and circular saws. Designs were created with standard board widths and lengths in mind, which minimizes waste. As for the non-woodworking projects, they are similarly easy to construct and employ equally simple assembly techniques.

For the more seasoned woodworkers among you, note that each project is completely adaptable to more sophisticated joinery and joining methods. That means your table saw, compound miter saw, pneumatic nailer, pocket screw jig, and soldering torch can get a workout, too.

Another thing you'll notice about some of the projects in *Garden Builder* is their adaptability. The raised miniature garden on page 100 for example, can also be used as a serving side table. Or consider the copper trellis on page 22, which can be used as a traditional plant support or a stand-alone garden feature, as can the garden obelisk on page 52. The kids' raised garden (page 96) makes a perfectly sized lettuce planter. Perhaps the pinnacle of adaptability is the modular, pest-proof garden on page 148, which can be made with or without pest-proof panels. It consists of boxes made in two different sizes that can be configured and stacked to suit any yard, no matter the size.

The most unique and interesting gardens consist of a little of everything, and so too does *Garden Builder*. From decorative focal points to helpful additions and everything in between, these projects are meant to the enhance the garden as well as our gardening experience. We hope their construction, their presence when completed, and the satisfaction of building them yourself provide you with great joy.

NOMINAL SIZE	ACTUAL SIZE
1×2	¾" × 1 ½"
1×3	¾" × 2 ½"
1×4	¾" × 3 ½"
1×6	¾" × 5 ½"
1×8	¾" × 7 ½"
2×4	1 ½" × 3 ½"
2× 6	1 ½" × 5 ½"
2×8	1 ½" × 7 ½"
2×10	1 ½" × 9 ½"

Lumber Issues

If you build the projects in this book according to the listed dimensions and wood species, construction should be relatively easy. You might run into difficulty, though, if you choose to adapt the plans to change the sizes of the projects. The problem here will stem from the fact that *nominal* lumber sizes are different than the *actual* sizes. Moreover, the actual sizes may vary depending on the lumber grade and species you buy.

The word nominal means "in name only." Although experienced woodworkers and carpenters are well aware of this fact, it can surprise beginning woodworkers to learn that a construction 2 × 4, for example, actually measures 1 ½ × 3 ½ inches. The reason for this has to do with the milling of the lumber. Although a 2 × 4 may arrive for its final finishing as a true 2 × 4, once it is planed down for sale, its dimension changes to its actual 1½ × 3½-inch dimensions.

This is true of pretty much any lumber you buy, no matter what the species. The difference between nominal and actual dimensions varies depending on the lumber grade and type, but it is always there. Fine-quality hardwoods have a very predictable variation—a 1 × 4, for example, is always ¾ × 3 ½ inches—but on rough-sawn cedar, the variation can be less precise. A 1 × 8 plank of rough cedar is assumed to be ¾ × 7 ¼ inches, but in actuality might be ⅞ × 7 ½ inches. And because many of the projects in this book are built with cedar, you have a good chance of running into measurement differences.

The moral here is that you will need to double check measurements for the parts when building the projects in this book. We've sized the elements based on standard assumptions for actual board sizes versus nominal, but there is a good chance that the rougher grade lumbers may be different than the normal actual dimensions.

While we're still discussing nominal board measurements, we need to consider board lengths as well. Don't assume a 6-foot board measures 6 feet long just because it's in the 6-foot bin at the lumberyard. Often, board stock measuring less than 8 feet are *drops*, or leftover cuts from a longer board. So that 6-foot board may measure up to an inch short. Because many of the projects featured in this book were designed to minimize material waste, measure the board lengths to make sure you're getting the full measurement.

Squaring Up a Project

Now let's say you've run the numbers, and you've implemented the formulas provided. You arrange your stiles and rails for assembly. You even clamp them all together. But when you're finished gluing and screwing the structure, the result is anything but *in square*. There's a quick trick to make sure all your angles are 90 degrees, and it goes like this: simply measure from one outside corner diagonally to its opposite corner, then repeat this same technique for the other two corners. If their measurements are the same, the structure is square. Be aware that the same technique can be used to square up a structure that is already assembled. In this case, bar clamps can be used to "rack" the structure into square.

Lumber Type

Although pressure-treated lumber may be used to construct many of the following projects, it is not advised to use pressure-treated lumber to construct planters and raised gardens that will be producing edibles. For those in which food will be grown, choose naturally rot-resistant wood species that are readily available to you. For us, that means rough-sawn western red cedar. If you don't already know what choices are available to you, rely on the expertise of the professionals at your local lumber yard for advice.

Weatherproofing Your Project

Keep in mind that even rot-resistant lumber—especially that which is 1 inch thick or less—can succumb to warping and cracking when it comes into direct contact with wet dirt for prolonged periods of time, such as when used for making planters. That's why it's best to coat them with some sort of waterproofing agent, such as brush- or spray-on liquid rubber. The first can be found in the roofing area of your local big box store, as it's sold to repair roof leaks. The spray-on version can usually be found in the paint aisle along with other aerosols. If using either of these products, always tape off and protect all surfaces which you do *not* want to rubberize.

Having used both the spray-on version and the brush-on version of liquid rubber, we find the spray-on versions work best when waterproofing the inside of terracotta pots. This is an especially important step when painting the outside of the pots. It may seem counterintuitive, but we prefer to paint the outside of the pot first and then, when the paint is fully dry, to tape off the exterior and spray the interior last. This is because tape—even the low-tack variety—will pull the cured rubber off the pot. On the other hand, our preferred waterproofing method for wooden planters is brush-on liquid rubber. Although it's more messy than its aerosol counterpart, it is much more cost effective.

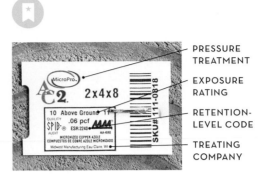

Pressure-treated lumber stamps list the type of preservative and the chemical retention level, as well as the exposure rating and the name and location of the treating company.

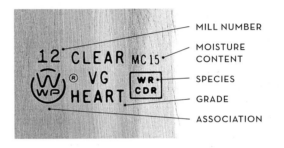

Cedar grade stamps list the mill number, moisture content, species, lumber grade, and membership association. Western red cedar (WRC) or incense cedar (INC) for decks should be heartwood (HEART) with a maximum moisture content of 15% (MC15).

TIP: *When waterproofing the inside of terracotta pots, paint the outside and top lip of the pots first. Then, when the paint is dry, tape and paper off the painted area and apply spray-on rubber last.*

Finishing Screw & Nail Holes

Because most of the joinery used in *Garden Builder* is glue-and-screw, you'll be left with noticeable screw holes. Although they need not be filled, you do have a few options if you want to do so. Three popular methods involve using glue and sawdust, epoxy wood filler, or handmade (or store-bought) wood plugs.

For the first method, you simply mix exterior wood glue with sawdust left over from your project cuts into a paste. Use it to overfill the screw holes and then sand it flat. It's an easy, very cost-effective technique, but isn't the most refined.

Epoxy wood filler is an excellent choice to fill screw holes, as it is incredibly durable and impervious to water. It's available in many colors that can be blended to better match the species of wood with which you are working. The third option—handmade or store-bought wood plugs—is the woodworker's choice for hiding screw holes; however, these definitely take planning and effort.

Copper

Besides wood, another material you'll see in some of the forthcoming projects is copper—specifically, copper pipe and fittings. We are using ordinary Type M rigid copper—the type sold at all hardware stores and home centers for residential plumbing use. For ease of assembly, the projects here utilize the very dependable 100 percent waterproof polyurethane glue to attach the various fittings to the pipes. But, if you happen to have the expertise and a soldering torch, soldering the fittings together is an excellent option. If you do choose the second method, try this old plumber's trick: wipe the outside of the joint while it's still hot with a wet rag to give the solder a nice shine.

Tools

The tools used to complete all of the projects in *Garden Builder* are of the standard variety and can be found in any home improvement or hardware store. Ease of construction should not preclude you from using more specialized tools, should you have them, to perform the tasks at hand. If you have a power miter saw or table saw, for example, by all means use that rather than a circular saw for your lumber-cutting tasks.

There are a few tools you might not yet have in your arsenal that will make your construction easier. The first are bar clamps. One clamp can act as an extra pair of hands. Two clamps equals two extra pairs of hands, and so on. They are ideal for holding the parts together while you concentrate on joining the parts. The bar clamps you'll see in the photos throughout this book are Quick-Grip clamps, though they are available in lots of different brand names. The most versatile lengths in regard to the projects featured here are the 2- and 3-foot varieties. No matter the length, these types of clamps are lightweight, easy to tighten and release, and are reasonably priced—which are the reasons we highly recommend them.

A variety of Quick-Grip clamps is a must-have for any woodworking shop.

Because several projects require you to mix cement, the second specialty tool to have on hand is a mixer paddle attachment for your drill. Yes, a stick can work for mixing up small, 5-gallon-pail-sized amounts of concrete, but a mixer paddle can do the job in minutes and will mix the concrete more thoroughly than a stick can. Plus, using a mixer paddle is easier physically as well.

You'll need to cut copper pipe for some of the projects featured in the decorative section. Yes, a hacksaw can be used to do this, but the cut will most likely have burrs and won't be square. For these reasons it's best to use a pipe/tubing cutter when cutting pipe. But not just any pipe cutter. Buy or borrow one that is considered heavy duty. They're not expensive—a good one might cost $20 to $30—and they'll make the job of cutting pipe much easier, faster, and cleaner than a $5 to $10 mini pipe cutter.

When it comes to pipe cutters, size matters. Skip the petite contraption on the right and go for the more robust option on the left. It will make your job much easier and your cuts more precise.

Keep Safety in Mind

Finally, whether you're a beginner or a seasoned woodworker, always work safely. Consult any and all operating manuals that accompany your equipment, and always wear protective gear such as dust masks, safety goggles/glasses, gloves, and hearing protection when necessary. Make sure all electrical cords are clear of blades and drive belts. If you respect your power tools by working smartly and carefully, they will provide you with the means to create projects you can proudly claim as your own creations.

The Projects

Concrete & Copper Stake Art

ALTHOUGH THIS PROJECT has an "official" title, around my house it has become lovingly referred to as "the donuts." One look and you can see why. Harder than its namesake but nearly as sweet, a single concrete donut can add interest to any garden spot, but two or more lends an organic effect, as if they sprouted up by seed. Unlike flowers, however, these copper and concrete confections are impervious to just about anything. So when the dry days of summer are wilting everything in sight, your concrete and copper donuts will look as fresh as ever.

A few notes to keep in mind before you start: keeping the concrete mix on the loose side will result in a smooth donut that's free of voids. Also, it helps to occasionally rotate the copper pipe while it's in the mold as the concrete cures, thereby making the removal of the pipe easier when it's time to de-mold.

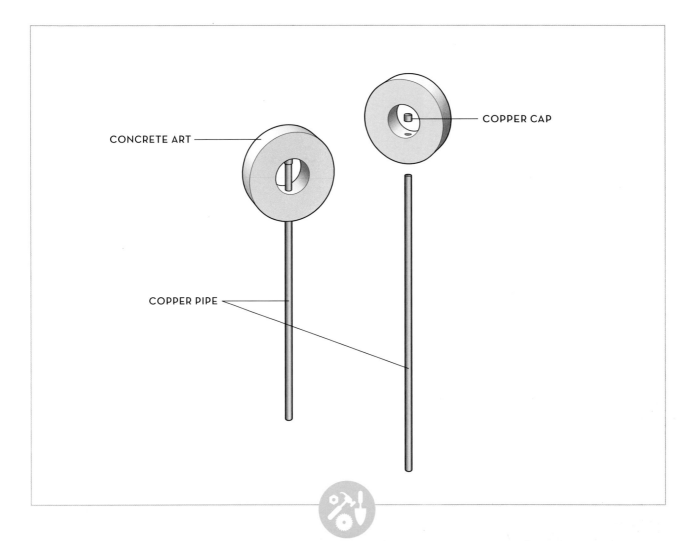

CONCRETE ART

COPPER CAP

COPPER PIPE

TOOLS & MATERIALS

- □ 4-quart plastic paint bucket, approximately 8½" × 7" high
- □ 1-quart round plastic container
- □ Tape measure
- □ Marking pen
- □ Utility knife
- □ Nonstick cooking spray
- □ Scrap piece of 2 × 6 or 2 × 8
- □ Drill
- □ 1½" screw

- □ Pail for mixing concrete
- □ Mixing stick or mixer paddle for drill
- □ Reinforced concrete
- □ Water
- □ Small garden trowel
- □ Particle mask, eye protection, latex or rubber gloves
- □ 1 × 2 scrap lumber to use as tamper
- □ Scrap boards to use as props

- □ Rubber mallet (optional)
- □ ¾" × 10' copper pipe (for three or four stakes)
- □ Copper tubing cutter
- □ ¾" copper cap (one for each stake made)
- □ ½" × 24" rebar (one per stake made)
- □ Hammer

Making Concrete &
Coopper Stake Art

1. Measure and mark both the 4-quart paint bucket and the 1-quart plastic container, 1¾ inches up from the bottom. Using a utility knife, cut a hole just large enough to accept the ¾" copper pipe at each of these marks.

2. Spray the inside of the bucket and the outside of the plastic container with nonstick cooking spray. Set the bucket on a scrap piece of 2 × 6 or 2 × 8.

3. Center the 1-quart container inside the bucket so that the side holes of the container are exactly aligned with the holes in the bucket. Drive a screw down through the bottom of the container, through the bottom of the bucket and into the scrap wood below. If you wish, you can insert the copper pipe in order to keep the holes aligned while you drive the screw.

4. Wearing gloves, mask, and eye protection, mix up enough concrete to fill the outside ring created between the pail and the container to a depth of approximately 5 inches. Keeping the mix on the looser side will make filling the donut easier.

5. Insert the copper pipe through each hole, bringing it into contact with the opposite inside surface of the container.

6. Using the garden trowel and tamping as you go, pour concrete evenly in the ring between the bucket and the container until the mixture comes up to the bottoms of the holes in the bucket container.

7 Tuck scrap boards under the long end of the copper pipe to keep it horizontal as the concrete cures. Continue to pour and tamp concrete into the ring until it covers the pipe by about 1 inch.

8 When the concrete has cured, remove the pipe and unscrew the screw at the center bottoms of the bucket and container.

9 Coax the center container from the concrete donut, and then free the donut itself from the bucket, using gentle taps with a rubber mallet, if needed.

10 Cut the ¾-inch copper pipe to desired length(s). For the project featured here, two lengths, one at 35 inches and one at 29 inches, were cut. Slide the copper pipe through the smaller hole at the bottom hole of the concrete donut until about 1½ inch is protruding from the large center hole.

11 Slip the copper cap onto the top of the pipe. Then continue to slide the entire copper assembly through the bottom hole until the cap touches the top of the donut's hole.

12 To install the project's stakes, hammer in the rebar at the desired location of the stake, and slip the stake's center copper pole over the rebar.

WARNING: *When installing rebar, beware of electrical wires, as well and any other utility services, buried underground.*

TIP: *If the pipe doesn't want to slide through the smaller hole, tap it with a rubber mallet.*

Concrete & Rebar Cattails

GARDENERS WHO LIVE near environments suitable for growing cattails have a love/hate relationship with them. Either they think they are a beautiful addition to the landscape or they think they're invaders of the weed variety. It's true that cattails can be prolific multipliers. That's in large part due to the velvety brown, spiked flowers that can blow out a staggering 220,000 seeds or more. Add to that their clone-producing rhizome root systems, and a few lowly cattails can become a colony of hundreds in no time flat.

Cattails made of concrete, on the other hand, mimic everything pleasing about the real thing without the worry of invasion. Their velvety texture comes from applying a skim coat of Portland cement mixed with silica sand, and the only thing their rebar stems will produce is rust, which, in this case, only adds interest.

TOOLS & MATERIALS

- ☐ Empty paper towel rolls (3)
- ☐ Masking tape
- ☐ Plastic container lids rescued from the recycling bin (3)
- ☐ Scissors
- ☐ 4 × 4 scrap lumber, about 12" long
- ☐ Drill

- ☐ 7/16" drill bit
- ☐ 3/8" × 3' rebar (3)
- ☐ Bucket, for mixing concrete
- ☐ Water
- ☐ Mixing stick or mixer paddle for drill
- ☐ Particle mask, eye protection, latex or rubber gloves

- ☐ Portland cement
- ☐ Silica sand
- ☐ 4 × 6-inch piece of cardboard, plastic, or wax-coated carton (optional)
- ☐ Hardwood dowel, approximately 3/8" to 1/2" thick (optional)

Making Rebar Cattails

1. Wrap each paper towel roll with masking tape to help maintain the structure of the cardboard roll. Cut three circles from the plastic lids to fit on one end of the paper towel rolls. With scissors, cut holes at the center of the circles to fit the circumference of the rebar.

2. Securely tape one circle to one end of each paper towel roll.

3. Drill three 7/16-inch holes through the scrap 4 × 4, as shown. Insert one section of rebar into each drilled hole.

4. With the plastic circle facing down, thread one paper towel roll onto each piece of rebar so that it is resting on the 4 × 4. Wearing gloves and mask, mix enough reinforced concrete to fill each paper towel roll. Opt for a looser mix rather than a stiffer one.

5. Use the 4 × 6-inch piece of cardboard, plastic, or wax-coated carton as a funnel to guide the concrete into the paper towel rolls. Continue filling the paper towel rolls with cement, using a small dowel as a tamper to ensure the cement is properly packed while making sure to keep the rebar centered in each roll.

6　When the concrete has cured (about 24 hours), peel off the tape and paper towel rolls.

7　With your gloves and mask on, mix up 1 part Portland cement to 2 parts silica sand (about 3 cups total). Add water to create a cake-frosting consistency. Using your gloved hands, use the mixture to apply a thin skim coat over the cattails, filling any voids and giving their surfaces a velvet-looking cattail texture.

WARNING: *When installing rebar, beware of electrical wires, as well and any other utility services, buried underground.*

Copper Trellis

TRELLISES, by their very nature, are meant to support climbing plants. Although this copper trellis can do just that, it aspires to do more, all by itself. Whether leaning against a wall or standing erect in a more natural backdrop, the trellis will add verticality to a garden of any style—traditional, modern, or even steampunk.

Assembled using polyurethane glue, the trellis is quite sturdy—especially as an "objet d'art" versus a plant support—but for those with the equipment and expertise, soldering the trellis's joints is an option as well.

Also, when choosing a tubing cutter to use for the project, don't skimp. Opting for a cutter labeled "heavy duty" will not only make the job of cutting pipe easier, it will make the cuts more uniform, as well.

CUT LIST

½" copper pipe

A. ½" × 13⅛" (6)

B. ½" × 12½" (4)

C. ½" × 9½" (4)

D. ½" × 6" (31)

E. ½" × 3" (16)

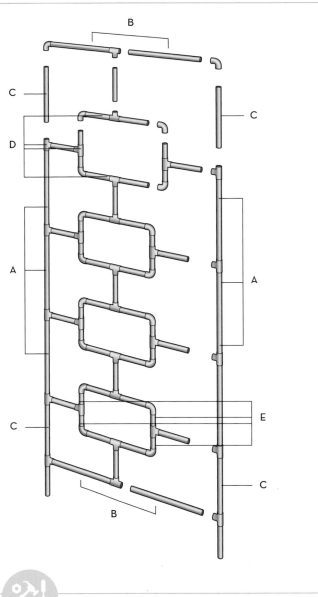

TOOLS & MATERIALS

- ☐ ½" × 10' copper pipe (4)
- ☐ Tape measure
- ☐ Marking pen
- ☐ Copper tubing cutter
- ☐ ½" copper tees (28)
- ☐ ½" copper elbows (18)
- ☐ Large piece of cardboard or paper
- ☐ Polyurethane glue
- ☐ Eye protection, gloves
- ☐ Water
- ☐ Spray bottle or sponge
- ☐ Utility knife
- ☐ ⅜" × 36" rebar (2)
- ☐ Hammer

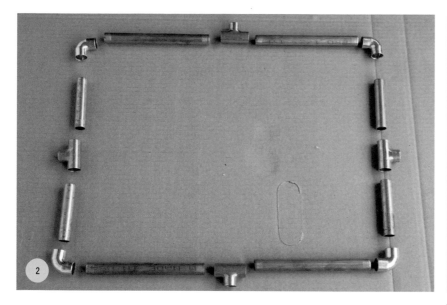

Making the Copper Trellis

1. Wearing eye protection and gloves, cut the copper pipe into the following lengths, using a copper tubing cutter:
   - ½ × 13 ⅛" (six pieces)
   - ½ × 12 ½" (four pieces)
   - ½ × 9 ½" (four pieces)
   - ½ × 6" (31 pieces)
   - ½ × 3" (16 pieces)

2. Find a level surface on which to work, protecting it with a large piece of cardboard or paper. Dry-fit all the components together on top of the cardboard, as shown in the illustration.

3. When the trellis shape is formed, glue the center motifs (the rectangles) together first, following the instructions on the polyurethane glue. Our product called for pre-wetting one side of the gluing surfaces first. (Using a spray bottle filled with water makes for quick and easy application.)

4 It is critical that when you glue the fittings together you make sure they are **flat against** your working surface and that each pipe is **fully inserted** into each fitting. Don't worry if the pipes adhere to the cardboard; a utility knife will scrape the pipes and fittings clean.

5 When the center motifs are cured (about 24 hours) glue and assemble the outer structure around the center motifs, starting with the top of the trellis and working down. Once again, make sure the fittings are flat against your working surface and that each pipe is fully inserted into each fitting.

6 Once the glue has dried (about 24 hours), use a utility knife to scrape cardboard and excess glue off the pipe. Let the entire outer structure cure overnight, and then install the trellis by hammering two pieces of rebar into the ground and slipping the trellis legs over the rebar.

WARNING: *When installing rebar, beware of electrical wires, as well and any other utility services, buried underground.*

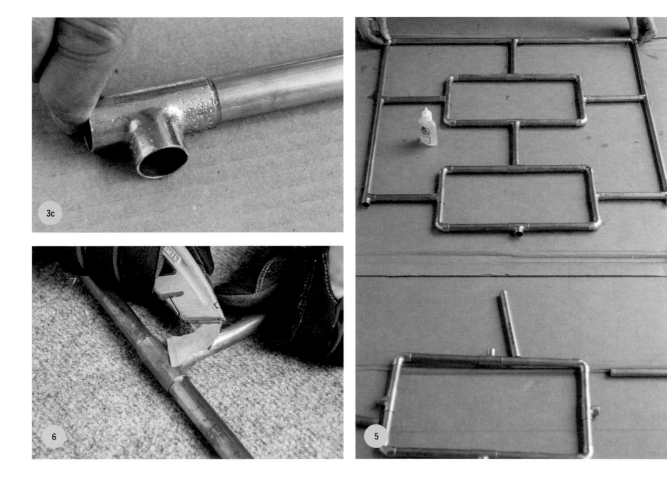

04

Deconstructed Concrete Gazing Ball

DO-IT-YOURSELF CRAFTERS have discovered they can make concrete spheres easily by using light fixture replacement globes as forms. The result is a rather subdued alternative to a gazing ball, which is why some people take the added step of applying mosaic tiles or flat marbles to the spheres to give them a bit of sparkle. There's an easier way to add shimmer to a concrete sphere, however, and it comes to us from the notion of deconstruction.

If you're a foodie, you'll be familiar with the term. If not, then all you need to know is that deconstructing a culinary dish is when its elements are taken apart and presented separately in a new and unique way. In this case, we're substituting proteins and starches with concrete and marbles and crushed mirrored glass. Although the parts are separate, together they are stunning, especially when struck by sunshine.

TOOLS & MATERIALS

- ☐ Glass ceiling light fixture replacement globe, approximately 8" diameter
- ☐ 6" flower pot
- ☐ Reinforced concrete
- ☐ Water
- ☐ 5-gallon bucket or other mixing container
- ☐ Eye protection, particle mask, latex or rubber gloves
- ☐ Mixing stick or drill with a mixing paddle
- ☐ Glass marbles
- ☐ Crushed mirrored candle filler (available in craft stores)
- ☐ Small putty knife
- ☐ 1 × 2 scrap for tamping
- ☐ Paper grocery bag
- ☐ Hammer
- ☐ Polyurethane glue (optional)

Making Your Deconstructed Gazing Ball

1. Set the globe, opening side up, inside the flower pot. Wearing safety gear, mix enough concrete and water per the manufacturer's instructions to fill the glass globe (but don't fill it yet). If you keep the concrete mix on the looser (wetter) side, it will help the concrete flow better between the marbles.

2. Mound two handfuls of marbles inside the globe, then scatter two handfuls of crushed mirror over the mound of marbles.

3. Using the putty knife as a "scoop," gingerly settle concrete over the marbles so as to disturb them as little as possible. Very gently tamp the concrete with the 1 × 2 as you pour in the concrete.

4. When the concrete is fully cured, place the globe inside a paper grocery bag.

5. Wearing eye protection and gloves, carefully tap the globe with a hammer to break away the glass.

NOTE: *Some of the marbles will fall away. If, however, you lose more marbles than you'd like, use a bit of polyurethane glue to reattach them.*

Faux Rock Cairn

THE FIRST TIME I saw a rock cairn was on the North Shore of Lake Superior in Minnesota. Stacks of smooth stones—affectionately called "lake rocks" by the locals—stacked on top of each other to form a blunted arrow pointing upward. Rather Zen in nature, the appearance of cairns erected in clusters is striking to see in such a natural setting, as it reminds those present of all those who have come before.

In ancient times, people formed cairns for a variety of reasons, such as marking a trail or a landmark. Traditionally they are made by carefully balancing rocks of various sizes in such a way that they won't topple over. That isn't as easy as it sounds, especially when faced with a limited selection of appropriately sized rocks to balance. This is probably why many garden centers sell pre-made cairns nowadays. These "cheater" versions consist of stones that have been predrilled and are fit over rods.

The beauty of making a *faux* rock cairn using concrete is that the final appearance, with the help of a little easy faux painting, looks very much like the real thing but at a fraction of the cost of garden center deceptions.

TOOLS & MATERIALS

- ☐ Plastic shopping bags
- ☐ Scissors
- ☐ Particle mask, eye protection, latex or rubber gloves
- ☐ Plastic tarp or drop cloth
- ☐ Portland cement
- ☐ Play sand
- ☐ Mixing bucket

- ☐ Mixing stick or mixer paddle for drill
- ☐ Putty knife
- ☐ String or twist ties
- ☐ Drill
- ☐ 7/16" carbide masonry drill bit
- ☐ 1 × 12 × 12" scrap wood
- ☐ Silica sand

- ☐ Flat acrylic craft paint in black, red, and off-white
- ☐ Empty spray bottle
- ☐ 3/8" rebar, 24" or 36" long (depending on height of cairn)
- ☐ Hammer

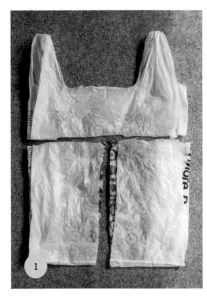

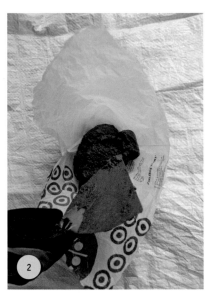

Making a Faux Rock Cairn

1. Cut the tops off the plastic shopping bags, and then cut them down the center, thereby creating two pieces with one original corner on each piece.

2. Wearing a particle mask, eye protection, and latex or rubber gloves, mix 1 part Portland cement to 2 parts sand to standard, medium consistency (not too dry or too wet). With a putty knife, drop a handful of the concrete into the corners of each plastic bag.

3. Draw the sides of the bag up and knot the top, making a cement "biscuit." Repeat the process to make biscuits of various sizes, 3 inches wide or larger. In our project, we made a total of ten stones, but you may vary as you wish to fit your rebar appropriately.

4. When the concrete biscuits have cured—about 24 hours or so—release them from their plastic cocoons and let them dry completely, as they quite likely will be damp. Don't worry that your biscuits look nothing like rocks at this point. That will soon be corrected.

5. When the biscuits have dried, drill holes through their centers, using a 7/16" masonry bit. To do this, position each biscuit on scrap wood and clamp or hold it in position with your feet. If the cement chips during the drilling process, don't worry; a skim coat will fix this.

6   Mix up 1 part Portland cement and 2 parts silica sand to a consistency of store-bought cake frosting to serve as a skim coat. Wearing rubber gloves, smooth handfuls of the skim coat all over the surface of the biscuits. Try to avoid the drilled holes, but if you happen to fill a hole with skim coat, use a screwdriver or dowel to unclog it.

7   Before you finish with the skim coat, take an assessment of the biscuits and choose one for the top of your cairn. (It'll probably be one of the smaller rocks.) Take your designated top stone and fill the drilled hole halfway with skim coat to hide the top hole.

8   After the skim coat has cured, it's time to make the biscuits look like rocks. Start by mixing 1 part of the darkest acrylic paint (in this case, black) with 1 part water in a spray bottle.

9　Spray the smoothed biscuits with a heavy hand, holding the spray bottle about 6 inches away from the rocks.

10　When you're satisfied with the coverage of the darkest paint, clean out the spray bottle and mix the same ratios of paint and water to the second darkest paint (in this case, red). This time, however, use a light hand and hold the bottle farther away from the rocks, about 12 inches. Repeat this step with the lightest paint color (in this case, an off-white paint).

TIP: *If you happen to spray too much of one color paint on the faux rocks, simply dab a damp paper towel on the excess paint to diminish it.*

11 When the paint is dry, find a place in the yard to install your cairn.

WARNING: *When installing rebar, beware of electrical wires, as well and any other utility services, buried underground.*

Use a hammer to insert the rebar just deep enough to accommodate all your faux rocks. You may need to thread the faux rocks onto the rebar and adjust the height as needed with the rocks in place. Don't install the top rock until you've established the appropriate height of the rebar. The faux rocks are quite durable, but you won't want to take a hammer to them. Although you'll want to have the largest of the rocks as the base, it's best to vary the sizes as you stack the rocks, as this provides the best visual effect.

TIP: *For long-lasting faux effect, wait approximately three to four weeks and apply cement sealer to your rocks.*

Fire Cube Tower

CUT LIST

Plywood form for cube

A. ½" × 7 ½" × 7 ½" for top (1)

B. ½" × 6" × 7 ½" for sides (2)

C. ½" × 6" × 8 ¾" for front and back (2)

Plywood for optional plinth

D. ½" × 6 ½" × 6 ½" for top (1)

E. ½" × 6 ½" × 18" for sides (2)

F. ½" × 7 ½" × 18" for front and back (2)

OUTDOOR FIREPLACES have become *de rigueur* when it comes to any landscape design. And if it's not a fireplace, then it's a coffee table with a fire pit at its center. True, both are lovely and have their place, but not everyone has the space—or the budget—to add one to their outdoor living areas.

Enter the fire column. Made of Portland cement and sand, the fire cube has the added feature of a glass sleeve, or what lantern manufacturers often refer to as a *globe*. The globe not only protects the flame from the breeze, it also gives the cube a finished and more polished look. By itself, the cube portion is small enough to sit on a table top, but to turn the fire cube into a statement piece, make the optional plinth and transform it into a fire column.

TOOLS & MATERIALS

- ☐ ½" × 2' × 4' plywood
- ☐ Tape measure
- ☐ Pencil
- ☐ Particle mask, eye protection, work gloves, latex or rubber gloves
- ☐ Circular saw or table saw
- ☐ Clamp
- ☐ Drill
- ☐ #8 × 1¼" screws
- ☐ 5"-diameter glass replacement lantern globe/sleeve (a 5" Coleman lantern replacement globe was used for this project)

- ☐ Corrugated cardboard
- ☐ Utility scissors
- ☐ Duct tape
- ☐ 1 can of Sterno Handy Wick
- ☐ Portland cement
- ☐ Play sand
- ☐ Water
- ☐ Mixing bucket
- ☐ Mixing stick or mixer paddle for drill
- ☐ 6" putty knife
- ☐ ⁷⁄₁₆" carbide masonry bit
- ☐ Crushed decorative stone
- ☐ Cooking spray

For the optional plinth:
- ☐ ½" × 2' × 4' exterior grade plywood
- ☐ Circular saw or table saw
- ☐ Tape measure
- ☐ Pencil
- ☐ Weather-resistant glue
- ☐ Hammer
- ☐ 1¼" finish nails
- ☐ Outdoor paint or stain
- ☐ Bristle or foam brush
- ☐ ⅜" × 24" rebar (2)

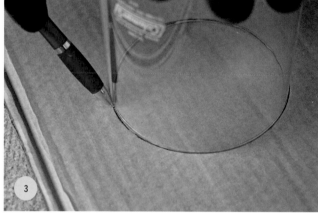

Making a Fire Cube Tower

1. Wearing safety gear, cut the plywood into the following quantities and dimensions, using a table saw or circular saw:
   - 7 1/2 × 7 1/2" (1)
   - 6 × 7 1/2" (2)
   - 6 × 8 3/4" (2)

2. Using 1 1/4" screws, attach the two 6 × 7 1/2-inch sides to the two 6 × 8 3/4-inch sides to form a perfect square. Then fit the 7 1/2 × 7 1/2-inch piece into the bottom of the square and screw it into place.

3. Using the globe as a pattern, trace and cut a circle from the cardboard.

4. Cut a strip of cardboard approximately the same height as the Sterno can. Trim the strip to fit the circumference of the glass globe.

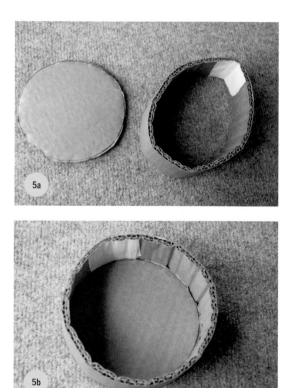

5 Use duct tape to tape the two ends of the strip together to form a ring. Then fit the cardboard circle into the ring and tape them together.

6 Apply duct tape to the entire cardboard assembly, including the outside of the circle. Make sure that the assembly will fit over one end of the lantern globe.

7 Spray the bottom and sides of the cardboard assembly with cooking spray (it should be completely covered in duct tape at this point), and center the assembly inside the plywood box, as shown.

8 According to manufacturer's instructions, mix 1 part Portland cement to 2 parts play sand with enough water to a slightly loose consistency. This will help create a cube with clean edges and a smooth finish. Using the putty knife, fill the box around the cardboard assembly with concrete. Make sure to maintain the position of the cardboard assembly as you fill the box. Continue to fill the box with concrete until it reaches the top edge of the box.

9   Next, use a 6" putty knife to smooth the top of the concrete.

10   When the concrete has cured—about 24 hours—unscrew the all sides of the box and release the concrete cube. Coax the cardboard assembly out, as well.

11   Use a drill and 7/16-inch bit to drill a drainage hole in the center of the circular cavity.

12   To make the optional plinth, cut the plywood into the following sizes and quantities:

- 1/2 × 6 1/2" × 18" (2)
- 1/2 × 7 1/2" × 18" (2)
- 1/2 × 6 1/2" × 6 1/2" (1)

Glue and nail the 7 1/2-inch lengths of plywood to the 6 1/2-inch lengths, creating the sides of a 7 1/2 × 18-inch box.

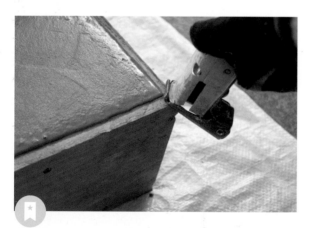

TIP: *Using a power hand tool that produces a significant amount of vibration, such as a reciprocating saw minus the blade, for example, move the tool along the edge of the concrete form. The vibration will help settle the concrete and thereby help eliminate voids.*

9

10a

10b

11

13 Slip the 6 ½ × 6 ½-inch piece of plywood into one end and glue and nail it into place.

14 Set the fire cube on top of the plinth and mark the wood beneath the drainage hole. Drill a 7/16-inch hole through the top of the plinth.

15 Paint or stain the plinth as desired (not pictured).

16 To prevent tipping, hammer the rebar into the ground where you'd like to display the fire column so that each length will be positioned in two opposite corners of the plinth. Then slip the plinth over the rebar.

WARNING: *When installing rebar, beware of electrical wires, as well and any other utility services, buried underground.*

17 Finally, set the globe inside the cavity and center the Sterno Handy Wick inside the globe. Sprinkle the decorative stone around and over the Sterno can.

12

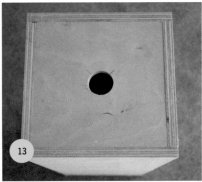

13

16a

16b

17

07

Whimsical Bottle Leaf Sculpture

½" copper pipe

- ½" × 6" (9)
- ½" × 12" (2)
- ½" × 18" (2)

THE FIRST TIME I heard mention of bottle sculptures was in Eudora Welty's short story, "Livvie," where the title character believes that "bottle trees kept evil spirits from coming into the house." The visual of a tree—a crape-myrtle tree in the case of "Livvie"—covered in bottles seemed like something out of a fairytale, not the American South.

More popular than ever, frameworks for today's bottle trees are most often constructed out of metal rather than tree limbs, as they were when they first came from the Caribbean via West Africa centuries ago. This project pays homage to the original bottle tree but doesn't combat evil spirits. Rather, it provides a whimsical focal point to the garden.

Assembled using polyurethane glue, this bottle tree is quite sturdy as it is. But for those with the equipment and expertise, soldering the sculpture's joints is an option, as well.

TOOLS & MATERIALS

- ☐ Tape measure
- ☐ Marking pen
- ☐ ½" × 10' copper pipe
- ☐ Pipe cutter
- ☐ ½" copper tees (4)
- ☐ ½" copper street elbows, 45 degrees (8)

- ☐ Large piece of cardboard, or something similar, to protect your working surface
- ☐ Polyurethane glue
- ☐ Water
- ☐ Sponge or spray bottle
- ☐ Eye protection, work gloves
- ☐ Decorative bottles (5)

- ☐ Hammer
- ☐ ½" rebar, 36" long
- ☐ 16- or 18-gauge copper wire
- ☐ Wire cutter and needle nose plier (optional)
- ☐ Assorted large glass or acrylic beads

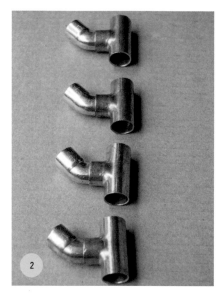

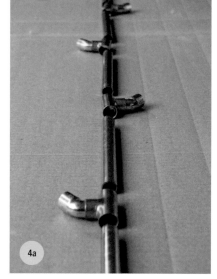

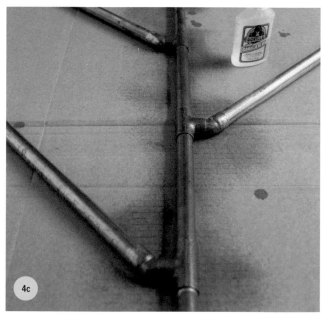

Making a Bottle Tree Sculpture

1. Don safety clothing and using the pipe cutter, cut nine pieces of copper pipe 6 inches long, two pieces 12 inches long, and two pieces 18 inches long.

2. Glue one end of four 45-degree elbows into the stem of each tee, following the instructions on the polyurethane glue. Our glue called for pre-wetting one side of the gluing surfaces first (using a spray bottle filled with water makes for quick and easy application). Push the tees and 45-degree elbow assemblies onto your working surface to ensure they are flat.

3. When the connections are cured (about 24 hours), glue an 18-inch length of copper pipe onto the bottom of one elbow/tee assembly so the 45-degree elbow is facing left.

4. Continue the center assembly by gluing on a 6-inch length of pipe and then a tee with the second 45-degree facing right. Continuing gluing on the remaining 6-inch lengths of pipe and the tees with the 45-degree elbows (facing alternately right and left.)

TIP: *Assembling the bottle tree in three gluing stages is the best way to ensure proper alignment of pipes and fittings; however, you could also glue the entire structure at one time as well.*

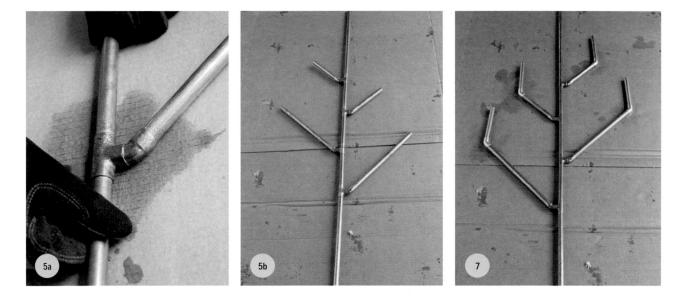

5 Glue two 12-inch lengths into each of the lower elbow/tee assemblies and two 6-inch lengths into each of the upper elbow/tee assemblies.

6 Glue the remaining 18-inch length to the top of the final tee. When gluing is complete, press the assembly firmly against your work surface to make sure all the fittings and pipe are flat.

7 After the glue has cured, glue a 45-degree elbow to the end of each arm, and then glue a 6-inch length into each elbow.

8 Optional: Using a needle nose plier, attach lengths of copper wire to the center trees. Slip beads onto the wire and secure the opposite ends to the pipe just below the lip of the bottle.

9 To install the bottle tree, drive the rebar into the ground with the hammer, and slip the center pipe over the rebar. Finish by slipping the five bottles onto branches of the tree.

WARNING: *When installing rebar, beware of electrical wires, as well and any other utility services, buried underground.*

TIP: *The polyurethane glue will cause the cardboard to stick to the bottle tree. Just use a utility knife to scrape the glue and material off the pipe.*

Bat Hotel & Pup Catcher

IMAGINE ADMIRING THE ONCOMING DUSK of a warm summer evening and noticing an object flying ungainly above the treetops. You realize the thing you thought might be a bird in distress is *actually* a bat. Now multiply that bat by three or six. If that sounds like the makings of a nightmare, it shouldn't—just one little brown bat can devour up to 1,000 mosquitos an hour. An hour! What with the mosquito-borne diseases lurking in the shady areas of our gardens, that alone should be reason enough to open a hotel just for them.

Much as all fine hotels, this establishment comes with sitting services for bat babies. Referred to as "pups," sometimes the babies fall out of their nesting area and become prey. A pup catcher, on the other hand, breaks their fall and gives them an opportunity to crawl back up to their nesting area. Slim and unobtrusive, this cozy bat hotel features a catcher that bat parents will surely appreciate.

CUT LIST

A. 1" × 2" × 18" for side spacers (2)

B. 1" × 2" × 14" for top spacer (1)

C. 1" × 3" × 14" for the roof (1)

D. 1" × 4" × 14" for the front and back of the pup catcher (2)

E. 1" × 4" × 3½" for the sides of the catcher (2)

F. ½" × 14" × 4½"

G. ½" × 14" × 14½"

H. ½" × 14" × 26" w/miters

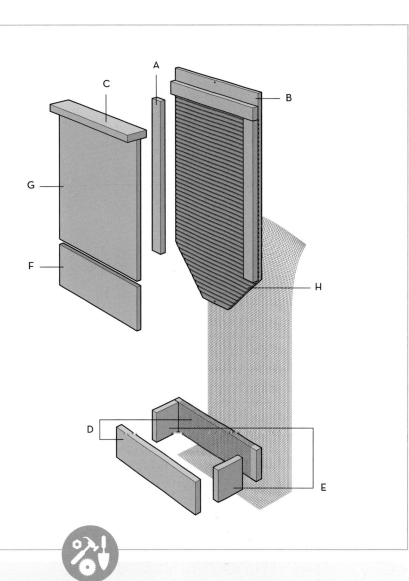

TOOLS & MATERIALS

- ☐ 1 × 2 × 6' cedar
- ☐ 1 × 3 × 4' cedar
- ☐ 1 × 4 × 4' cedar
- ☐ ½" ACX exterior plywood, 4' × 4' sheet
- ☐ Tape measure
- ☐ Pencil
- ☐ Particle mask, eye protection, hearing protection, work gloves

- ☐ Circular saw, miter saw, or table saw
- ☐ Clear exterior caulk
- ☐ Caulk gun
- ☐ Exterior stain (opt for black if you live in cool regions, mid-tones for mild regions, and white or light tones for hot regions)

- ☐ Application bristle or foam brush
- ☐ Hammer
- ☐ 1" finish nails
- ☐ 1 ½" finish nails
- ☐ Pet-resistant screening
- ☐ Scissors
- ☐ Stapler
- ☐ ⅜" staples

3a

3b

Making a Bat Hotel

1. Wearing safety gear, cut wood into the following lengths:
   - 1 × 2 × 18" for side spacers (2)
   - 1 × 2 × 14" for top spacer (1)
   - 1 × 3 × 14" for the roof (1)
   - 1 × 4 × 14" for the front and back of the pup catcher (2)
   - 1 × 4 × 3 ½" for the sides of the pup catcher (2)

2. Cut a strip off the plywood sheet to 14" wide, then cut that piece into three lengths measuring 26 inches, 14 ½ inches, and 4 ½ inches long. (The 26-inch piece will be the back of the bat house, the 14 ½-inch piece will be the upper section of the front, and the 4 ½-inch piece will be the lower section of the front.)

3. With a pencil, mark a point 5 inches up from the lower edge of the 26-inch long piece of plywood and a point 5 inches in from the lower edges of the back. Connect the points with a line, creating 45-degree corners. Repeat this marking procedure on the opposite side, and then saw off these corners with a circular saw.

4

4 Set the blade on your circular saw at a depth of 1⁄16 inch and cut a series of grooves across the back of the bat house at 1⁄2-inch intervals starting at the bottom, with the last groove positioned about 2 inches from the top edge. (An edge guide on your circular saw will make this job easier.)

5 Stain all the pieces of the bat hotel, front and back. After the stain has dried, lay the interior spacers (wide side facing you) onto the interior of the back. Apply caulk, then affix the spacers to the interior back of the bat house and attach with 1-inch finish nails.

6 Apply caulk to the front of the spacers, then position the front two sections of the bat house to the spacers and attach with 1 1⁄2" finish nails, leaving a 1⁄2-inch gap between the top section and the bottom section.

7 Run a bead of caulk at the top of the bat house.

5a

5b

6

7

8   Nail on the roof with 1 ½-inch nails.

9   Glue and nail the front and back of the pup catcher, creating an open-bottom box.

10 Cut two pieces of pet-resistant screening, one 14 × 36 inches and the other 10 × 12 ½ inches. Wrap the smaller piece of screening around the inside face of one of the longer sides of the pup catcher and staple it at the back as shown. (Installing the screening in this way gives any fallen pups a way to crawl up to the top of the box.)

11 Staple one end of the longer piece of screening so it covers one open end of the pup catcher. Turn the assembly on its front and staple the screening to the backside of the pup catcher. (The screening will overlap onto the previously installed screening.) The result will be an open-topped box that will catch fallen pups who can then climb back up the screening to return to the bat hotel.

12 Finally, staple the selvage edge of the screening to the bottom back of the bat hotel so there is approximately 24 inches separating the opening from the top lip of the pup catcher.

13 Install your bat house and pup catcher facing south to southeast, so it is 10 to 15 feet above ground. If possible, mount it on a metal pole to protect it from predators; however, a limbless tree trunk will also suffice. Because the pup catcher is made of pet-resistant screening, it may accumulate guano, which means it may need to be cleaned every now and then.

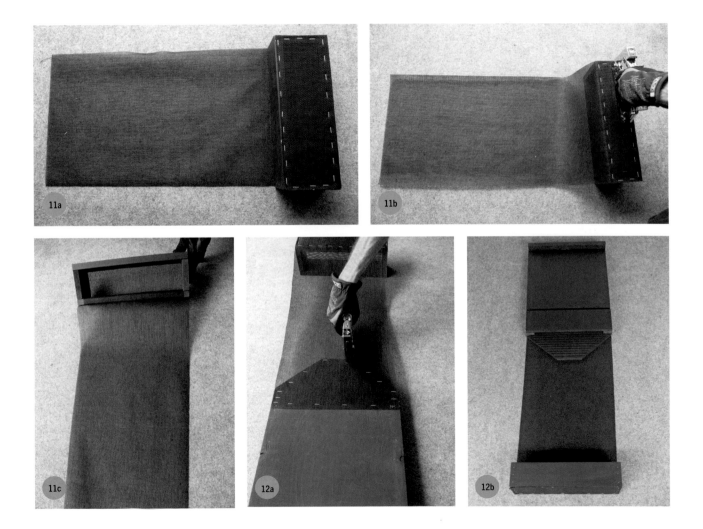

Garden Obelisk

OBELISKS BY DEFINITION are four- sided "monolithic pillars" that "terminate in a pyramid," or so Merriam-Webster tells us. Their presence can anchor a focal point in the garden, provide verticality, and add an element of elegance.

The garden obelisk featured here does all that, and even more. A true multitasker, it provides a structure for climbing plants and also happens to have a mirrored glass finial that serves as a gazing ball. If you want, you can paint the obelisk a bright color and forgo the climbing flower companion entirely for a low maintenance yet lively addition to the garden.

The option of creating the mirrored glass finial is an easy step that only requires finding an appropriate hollow glass ball. We found the one used in this project, which measures 4 inches in diameter, at a home decorating store. Usually used in multiples as bowl or platter fillers, such decorative spheres are perfect for creating finial gazing balls.

CUT LIST

A. 2" × 2" × 13" (10)

B. 2" × 2" × 16" (10)

C. 2" × 2" × 66" (4)

D. 2" × 2" × 14" mitered at 45° at each end (4)

E. 2" × 2" × 2 ⅛" for the top finial piece (1)

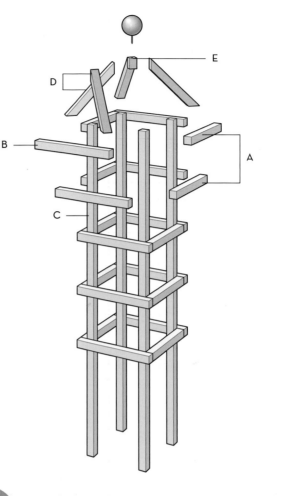

TOOLS & MATERIALS

- ☐ 2" × 2" × 8' pressure-treated or naturally weather-resistant lumber (8)
- ☐ Tape measure
- ☐ Pencil
- ☐ Particle mask, eye protection, hearing protection, work gloves
- ☐ Circular saw, miter saw, or table saw

- ☐ Bar clamps
- ☐ Drill
- ☐ #8 pilot/countersink bit
- ☐ #8 × 2 ½" triple-coated deck screws
- ☐ #10 pilot/countersink bit
- ☐ #9 × 3" triple-coated deck screws
- ☐ Exterior wood glue

- ☐ 2" finish nails
- ☐ Hammer
- ☐ Fabricated finial (optional)
- ☐ Portland cement
- ☐ Play sand
- ☐ Wood filler (optional)

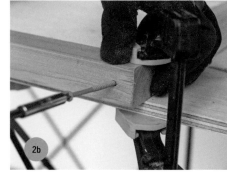

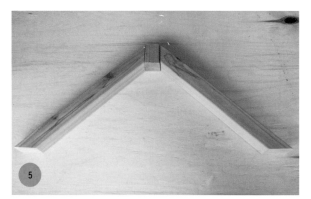

Making a Garden Obelisk

(1) Don safety gear and cut the 2" × 2" into the following lengths:

- 2 × 2 × 13" (10)
- 2 × 2 × 16" (10)
- 2 × 2 × 66" (4)
- 2 × 2 × 14" mitered at 45 degrees at each end (4)
- 2 × 2 × 2" for the top finial piece (1)

(2) Drill pilot holes and use 3" screws to assemble a frame with two 16-inch lengths onto two 13-inch lengths. Repeat to create the five frames. With the 16-inch pieces overlapping the 13-inch pieces, the frames will be exactly square.

(3) Next, attach one 66-inch long board into each of the corners of one of the frames to create legs. To do this, start at the end of one of the 66-inch boards, designating it as the top of the obelisk. Place the frame flush with the top of the leg; clamp together, if desired. Drill a countersunk pilot hole and attach the frame to the leg at one corner, using 2 ½" screws. Repeat for the other three legs/corners of the frame.

(4) Measure down 9 inches from the bottom of the first frame and attach the next frame, again using 2 ½" screws driven through countersunk pilot holes. Repeat for the remaining three frames.

(5) Attach two of the opposing mitered pieces to the 2-inch piece of wood, using glue and 2" finish nails. Attach the remaining two opposing mitered pieces to the 2-inch piece of wood, creating a four-legged pyramid shape.

(6) When the glue has set, attach the top pyramid assembly to the top of the obelisk with glue and 2" finish nails driven into the legs. Cover nail holes, if desired.

Optional Finial

1. The trick to fabricating a finial is finding a decorative object that you can fill with concrete. In this case, the ball used to create the finial came from a national home decor store. The mirrored glass ball has a hole at the bottom covered by a rubber plug.

2. To convert the ball to a finial, remove the plug and nestle the ball into a small terracotta flowerpot to keep the hole pointed up.

3. Fill the ball with a loose mix of Portland cement, play sand, and water. We used a cut-off length of plastic bottle as a makeshift funnel to direct the concrete mix into the ball.

4. Tamp with a wooden dowel to make sure the ball is completely filled with concrete mix.

NOTE: *For brevity's sake, when instructions state "attach," the step includes the added suggestion of drilling appropriately sized pilots and countersinks before installing screws.*

5. After the glass ball is filled, use a paper towel to clean off any concrete from its exterior. Then, insert a ¼ × 3" hex-head lag screw about halfway into the concrete through the hole.

6. Drill a hole into the center of the obelisk's top pyramid assembly, then screw the new mirrored finial into place.

Harvest Boxes

ALTHOUGH THESE BOXES are made to fit inside the vertical harvest pantry featured on page 168, they are also very useful as a solo act. Use them for harvesting your own garden, or take them to any "pick your own" grove when berries and apples are in season. And since the boxes are extremely sturdy, you don't have to worry about them collapsing under the weight of your harvest. Plus, they have generous handholds that lend a solid, old-time feeling that outrivals any commercial basket you can buy.

It's best to make these boxes in pairs, especially if you're building the accompanying vertical harvest pantry, as two of these boxes fit perfectly side by side on each of the pantry's shelves.

You can use almost any lumber for these boxes, except for pressure-treated lumber, which is impregnated with chemicals that are best not used with any container that will hold edibles.

CUT LIST

A. 1" × 4" × 10 ½" for the bottom of the box (3)

B. 1" × 4" × 13" for the front and back of the box (4)

C. 1" × 8" × 10 ½" for the ends of the box, with the handholds (2)

TOOLS & MATERIALS

- ☐ 1 × 4 × 8' lumber (2)
- ☐ 1 × 8 × 4' lumber (1)
- ☐ Tape measure
- ☐ Pencil
- ☐ Particle mask, eye protection, hearing protection, work gloves
- ☐ Circular saw, miter saw or table saw
- ☐ Drill

- ☐ 1" spade bit or Forstner bit
- ☐ Ruler or straightedge
- ☐ Jigsaw
- ☐ Wood rasp
- ☐ 60-grit sandpaper
- ☐ Glue
- ☐ Bar clamps
- ☐ 2" finish nails
- ☐ Hammer

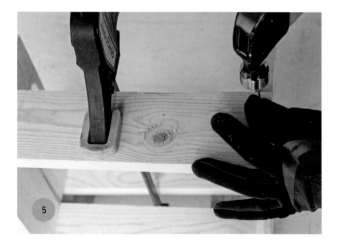

Making a Harvest Box

1. Don safety gear and cut the boards into the following lengths for each harvest box:
   - 1 × 4 × 10 ½" bottom pieces (3)
   - 1 × 4 × 13" front and back pieces (4)
   - 1 × 8 × 10 ½" end pieces (2)

   On the two end pieces, drill two 1-inch holes, 6 inches up from the bottom and 3 ¼ inches in from each side.

2. Using a ruler or straightedge, draw two lines from one hole to the other, as shown, to outline the handle openings.

3. Cut along the marked line using a jigsaw to fashion the handholds.

4. Use a wood rasp to round off the edges of the handholds, and then further smooth them with 60-grit sandpaper.

5. Apply glue and clamp two 1 × 4 × 13-inch boards flush with the bottom edges of the two end pieces with the handholds. Secure the joints by driving two nails in each end joint.

TIP: *Use a couple of scrap pieces of wood to raise the assembly, thereby establishing clearance for the bar clamp.*

6. Remove the clamp and repeat with the other two 1 × 4 × 13-inch boards, attaching them flush with the top edges of the two handhold end pieces.

7. Slip the three 10 ½-inch boards inside the bottom of the box, spacing them evenly apart, with a ¼-inch gap between boards. Use glue and nails to secure the bottom boards in place.

11

Kids' Potting Bench

IT SEEMS THAT the best time to get a child interested in gardening is when they still don't mind getting dirty. Add to that the magic of watching the seeds they plant grow into beautiful flowers or herbs, and you might get them hooked on gardening for the rest of their lives.

If, however, the gardening gene has skipped a generation and you need an additional incentive to encourage playing with dirt, then this potting bench is a must-build. Perfectly sized for little hands, the potting bench features a lift-off top and lower shelf to store gardening supplies. Install hooks on the side to hang kid-sized hand tools, and your little gardener's green thumb will turn absolutely emerald.

Although we built our potting bench with cedar, any weather-resistant lumber will work. Because children will be using the bench, however, we suggest avoid using pressure-treated wood because of its chemical content.

CUT LIST

A. 2" × 2" at 23 ⅞" long for the legs (4)

B. 1" × 8" at 17 ½" long for sides of potting box (2)

C. 1" × 8" at 20" long for front and back of potting box (2)

D. 1" × 4" at 17 ½" long for inside bottom of potting box (4)

E. 1" × 4" × 20" for the top of potting box (5)

F. 1" × 2" at 15 ¼" long for inside front and back cleats of potting box (2)

G. 1" × 2" at 14 ½" long for inside side cleats of potting box (2)

H. 1" × 2" × 17 ¼" for underside battens of the top of the potting box (2)

I. 1" × 2" × 18" for underside batten of the top of the potting box (1)

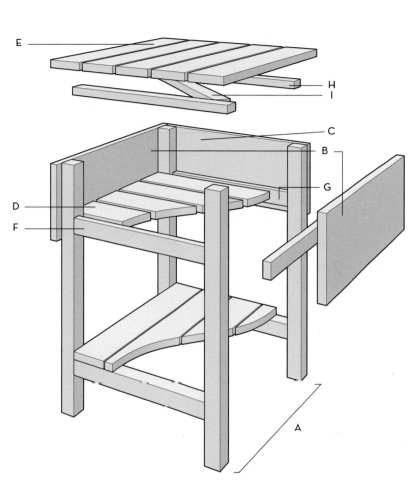

TOOLS & MATERIALS

- ☐ 1 × 2 × 8' cedar (2)
- ☐ 1 × 4 × 8' cedar (1)
- ☐ 1 × 4 × 10' cedar (1)
- ☐ 1 × 8 × 8' cedar (1)
- ☐ 2 × 2 × 8' cedar (2)
- ☐ Tape measure
- ☐ Pencil

- ☐ Particle mask, eye protection, hearing protection, work gloves
- ☐ Circular saw, miter saw, or table saw
- ☐ Hand sander
- ☐ 80-grit sandpaper
- ☐ 24" bar clamps (2)

- ☐ Exterior wood glue
- ☐ Drill
- ☐ #8 pilot/countersink bit
- ☐ #8 × 1 ¼" screws
- ☐ #8 × 2" screws
- ☐ Wood filler (optional)

NOTE: *For brevity's sake, when instructions state "attach," the step includes the added suggestion of drilling appropriately sized pilots and countersinks before installing screws.*

Making a Kids' Potting Bench

1. Don safety gear and saw the boards into the following quantities and lengths:
   - 2 × 2 × 23 ⅞" (legs) (4)
   - 1 × 8 × 17 ½" (sides) (2)
   - 1 × 8 × 20" (front and back) (2)
   - 1 × 4 × 17 ¼" (inside bottom slats) (4)
   - 1 × 4 × 20" (top) (5)
   - 1 × 2 × 15 ¼" (inside front and back cleats) (2)
   - 1 × 2 × 14 ½" (inside side cleats) (2)
   - 1 × 2 × 17 ¼" (underside battens) (2)
   - 1 × 2 × 18" (underside batten) (1)

2. Start by sanding any rough or splintering areas of the wood. Clamp the front and back to the two sides of the planter.

3. Drill countersunk pilot holes about 1 inch down from the top and 1 inch up from the bottom and ⅜ inch from the outside edge, then use glue and 2" screws to join the front and back to the sides.

4 Designate one side of the box as the "top", then place this side face down. Position one of the four 2 × 2 legs at one of the corners of the bench so that it is ⅛ inch down from the top of the planter. Clamp the leg and then glue and attach the leg into place, using 2" screws. Repeat for the remaining three legs.

5 Glue and attach one of the long cleats to the inside front bottom edge of the planter using 1 ¼" screws. Repeat for the second long cleat.

6 Grab a scrap piece of 1 × 4 or 1 × 8 and attach it flush with the bottom edge of the bench, using it as a spacer to determine the depth of the shorter cleat. With the spacer in position, attach the shorter cleat into place.

7 Attach the four bottom slats to the inside the bench, using 1 ¼" screws driven into the longer cleats.

8 Measure the space between the front and back legs just below the potting bench box. Cut two 2 × 2s to this length for the bottom shelf stringers. Clamp the stringers in place between the legs, about 6 inches up from the bottom of the legs. Attach the stringers by driving 3" screws through the legs and into the stringers. Note: When attaching the stringers, you may need to pull the legs in slightly to guarantee verticality.

9 Cut four pieces of 1 × 4 equal to the outside dimensions of the legs. Position these boards so they are evenly spaced across the stringers, then attach them to the stringers with 1 ¼" screws.

10 Evenly space the bench top boards on a level surface, sanded side down, so they form a 20 × 19 ¼-inch rectangle. Attach the 17 ¼-inch underside battens to the top boards with 1 ¼" screws positioned 2 ⅜ inches in from the cut ends of the top boards and centered side to side.

11 Attach the 18-inch underside batten to the underside of the top boards diagonally between the outside battens to prevent the top from racking. Then fit the top of the box onto the box itself. If desired, fill the screw holes as described on page 10.

10

11a

11b

Tiered Drying Rack

HERBS, LIKE VEGETABLE GARDENS, can overwhelm us with a prolific crop. Luckily, preserving the former is much easier than preserving the latter. Herbs—especially oregano, thyme, rosemary, sage, lavender, mint, and lemon balm—are conducive to air-drying. Flowers, their petals, and some plants can be dried too. Good options are roses, sunflowers, statice, baby's breath, and ornamental grasses.

A three-tiered herb drying rack offers plenty of room to preserve your harvests, and it looks great while doing so. Although flowers may be placed directly on the individual screens when drying, we suggest using squares of flour sack cloth to line the screens when drying herbs. Besides keeping them off the screen, the cloth keeps bits of herbs from falling through the mesh as they dry, making cleanup much easier.

As for when to harvest herbs and flowers for drying, it's best to pick them in the morning after any dew has evaporated.

CUT LIST

Wood

A. 1" × 2" × 15" (12)

B. 1" × 2" × 18" (6)

C. 1" × 2" × 12" (6)

Screen

D. 14 ½" × 17 ½" (3)

Doweling

E. ¾" × 3" (12)

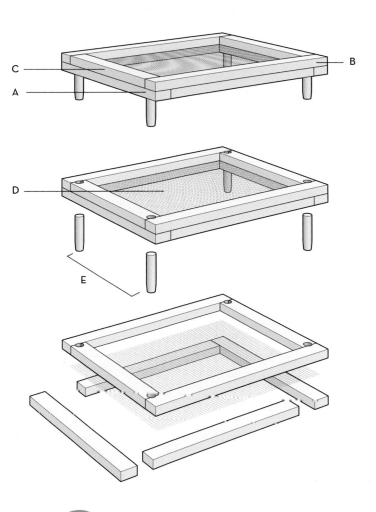

TOOLS & MATERIALS

- ☐ 1 × 2 × 10' select pine (4)
- ☐ Tape measure
- ☐ Pencil
- ☐ Particle mask, eye protection, work gloves
- ☐ Circular saw, miter saw, or table saw
- ☐ Bar clamps

- ☐ Aluminum screening
- ☐ Utility scissors
- ☐ Stapler
- ☐ ¼" staples
- ☐ Wood glue
- ☐ Drill
- ☐ #8 pilot/countersink bit
- ☐ #8 × 1 ¼" screws

- ☐ Scrap piece of plywood, 15 × 18"
- ☐ ¾" Forstner bit
- ☐ Masking tape
- ☐ ¾" × 4' dowel
- ☐ Handsaw
- ☐ 60-grit sandpaper
- ☐ Orbital or palm sander
- ☐ Flour sack towels

NOTE: *Each tier of the drying rack will consist of four 15-inch pieces, two 18-inch pieces, and two 12-inch pieces of 1 × 2.*

Making a Tiered Drying Rack

1. Don safety gear and cut the 1 × 2 lumber into the following lengths and quantities:
   - 1 × 2 × 15" (12)
   - 1 × 2 × 18" (6)
   - 1 × 2 × 12" (6)

2. Lay out and clamp together two 18-inch pieces with two 12-inch pieces between them, fashioning a frame.

3. Cut the screening into three pieces, each 14 ½ × 17 ½ inches. Staple the screening onto the frame's face.

TIP: *It's best to staple each corner of the screen into place first, and then staple three staples down each side between the corners.*

NOTE: *For brevity's sake, when instructions state "attach," the step includes the added suggestion of drilling appropriately sized pilots and countersinks beforehand.*

4 Apply a healthy bead of glue down each side of the frame on top of the screening.

 5 Arrange the remaining 15-inch pieces over the screen, and clamp into place.

6 Use screws to attach the 15-inch pieces into the wood below, securing the screening between them. Install one screw at each corner and two screws 2 inches from the first screw, for a total of three screws per corner.

 7 Drill a ¾-inch hole in each corner of the scrap piece of plywood, 1 ¾ inches in from the long (18 inch) side of the frame and ¾ inch in from the short (15 inch) side of the frame, creating a template.

TIP: *Mark one side of the template as the upper side.*

8 Center and clamp the template, right-side up, onto the *screwed side* of one of the frames. (The screwed side will function as the bottom of each frame.) Check to make sure you **do not** see any screw heads in the holes of the template.

9 Use masking tape to mark a depth on your drill bit of approximately ⅝ inches. Drill ¾-inch holes through the holes in the template and down into the screened frame until you reach the masking tape marking on the drill bit.

10 Unclamp the template, flip the frame over, and repeat. Repeat steps 8 to 10 for a second frame. For the third and final frame, drill holes on the *screwed side only*, as this will function as the top of the herb dryer.

11 Using a handsaw, cut the dowel into 12 lengths of 3 inches each.

12 Glue the dowels into the holes on the screwed side of the frames.

 13 While the glue is still wet, nest the dowel legs into the holes in the frame below to ensure the legs are vertical to the holes above.

 14 When the glue has cured, use 60-grit paper and an orbital or palm sander and sand the dowel legs into a gentle taper, checking for ease of fit into the holes on the top of the individual frames.

10

11

12

13

Vertical Corner Garden

IF YOU CHECK the exterior of your home, you probably have an inside corner or two that isn't doing much of anything. This vertical corner garden is the answer to an inside corner's dream. Used for flowers or even herbs, it's a perfect choice to occupy those underutilized spots. Its verticality is especially beneficial to help break up the horizontal nature of a deck or balcony.

Built from a series of four wooden boxes attached to a 4 × 4 pillar, this corner garden can be freestanding in some locations, but for greater stability, you might want to anchor the post to a wall.

Don't let the precise fits necessary to build this project intimidate you. Just follow the old adage, "measure twice and cut once" while building it and you'll be fine.

CUT LIST

Set #1:

A. 1" × 12" × 14 ¾" for 2 inside sides and 1 bottom piece (3)

B. 1" × 12" × 16 ¼" for 2 outside sides (2)

C. 1" × 4" × 11 ¼" for 1 bottom piece (1)

Set #2:

D. 1" × 10" × 12 ¾" for 2 inside sides and 1 bottom piece (3)

E. 1" × 10" × 14 ¼" for 2 outside sides (2)

F. 1" × 4" × 9 ¼" for 1 bottom piece (1)

Set #3:

G. 1" × 8" × 10 ¾" for 2 inside sides and 1 bottom piece (3)

H. 1" × 8" × 12 ¼" for 2 outside sides (2)

I. 1" × 4" × 7 ¼" for 1 bottom piece (1)

Set #4:

J. 1" × 6" × 9" for 2 inside sides and 1 bottom piece (3)

K. 1" × 6" × 10 ½" for 2 outside sides (2)

L. 1" × 4" × 5 ½" for 1 bottom piece (1)

M. 4" × 4" × 64" (1)

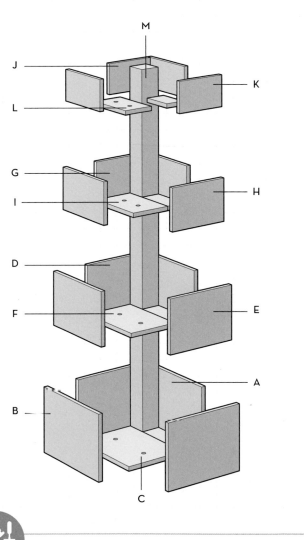

□ 1 × 12 × 8' cedar (1)
□ 1 × 10 × 8' cedar (1)
□ 1 × 8 × 8' cedar (1)
□ 1 × 6 × 8' cedar (1)
□ 1 × 4 × 8' cedar (1)
□ 4 × 4 × 6' cedar (1)
□ Scrap piece of 4 × 4
□ Tape measure
□ Pencil

□ Particle mask, eye protection, hearing protection, work gloves
□ Circular saw, miter saw, or table saw
□ Hand sander
□ 100-grit sandpaper
□ Bar clamps
□ Hammer
□ Drill
□ #8 pilot/countersink bit

□ #8 × 2" triple-coated deck screws
□ Exterior wood glue
□ ½" drill bit
□ Wood rasp (optional)
□ Spray-on rubber sealant, if using the planter for flowers only
□ Epoxy wood filler (optional)

Building a Vertical Corner Garden

1. Don safety gear and cut the boards into the following quantities and lengths. (Keep in mind that treating them as *sets* and keeping them together as sets will aid in construction later.)

   Set #1:
   - 1 × 12 × 14 ¾" (2 short sides and 1 bottom piece) (3)
   - 1 × 12 × 16 ¼" (sides) (2)
   - 1 × 4 × 11 ¼" (bottom piece) (1)

   Set #2:
   - 1 × 10 × 12 ¾" (2 short sides and 1 bottom piece) (3)
   - 1 × 10 × 14 ¼" (sides) (2)
   - 1 × 4 × 9 ¼" (bottom piece) (1)

   Set #3:
   - 1 × 8 × 10 ¾" (2 short sides and 1 bottom piece) (3)
   - 1 × 8 × 12 ¼" (sides) (2)
   - 1 × 4 × 7 ¼" (bottom piece) (1)

   Set #4:
   - 1 × 6 × 9" (2 short sides and 1 bottom piece) (3)
   - 1 × 6 × 10 ½" (sides) (2)
   - 1 × 4 × 5 ½" (bottom piece) (1)
   - 4 × 4 × 64" (support post) (1)

2. Starting with any one of the sets, use glue and screws to join two long sides to two short sides. The short sides should be positioned between the long sides, creating a square box. On the smaller boxes, drive two screws in each joint; on the larger boxes, use three screws.

3. Using the scrap 4 × 4 to help with placement, tuck the bottom pieces inside the box, trimming them to fit, if necessary.

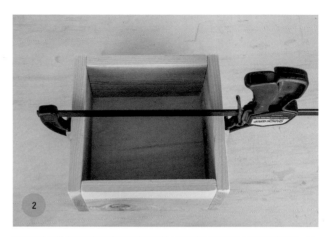

NOTE: *For brevity's sake, when instructions state "attach," the step includes the added suggestion of drilling appropriately sized pilots and countersinks before installing screws.*

4   Remove the scrap 4 × 4. Glue and clamp the larger bottom piece into position to ensure it is snug against the side. Using 2" screws, attach the bottom board along all three adjoining sides of the box.

5   Glue and clamp the smaller bottom board into position, making sure it is snug against the side. With 2" screws, secure it in position along the adjoining two sides of the box. Drill two ½-inch holes through the bottom of the box for drainage.

6   Repeat steps 2 through 6 for the other box sets. Apply waterproofing to the interior of each box as described on page 9, if desired.

7   When waterproofing is dry, slip the largest box over the 4 × 4 support post until the box is flush to the ground. If the box is too snug, use a wood rasp to slightly widen the bottom opening for a custom fit. Clamp the box to the support posts, and use 2" screws to secure the box to the post.

8   Repeat for the other boxes, from largest to smallest, spacing them about 10¼ inches apart. The lip of the top box should be flush with the top of the support post. Fill the screw holes with wood filler as described on page 10, if desired.

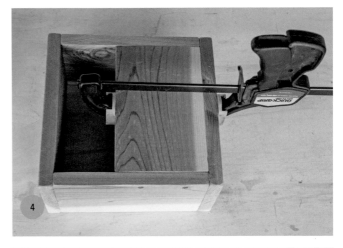

14

Bee-Friendly Planter

BEE FRIENDLY! Signs proclaiming the imperative are popping up everywhere in our neighborhood. It's hard to argue against it. Bees are our best buds when it comes to the garden, for where would we be without bees? Hungry, that's where. For this reason, a planter friendly to bees seems like a perfect addition to any gardener's to-build list.

The planter featured here has a side compartment that holds bee-friendly housing whereas the planter compartment itself is filled with bee-friendly flowers. In this case, white alyssum; the petunias add color and attract hummingbirds.

Although the housing material was chosen to attract docile mason bees, it's best to approach the planter from the closed side and keep it nearer the garden rather than the patio or deck so as not to disturb the pollinators at work.

CUT LIST

A. 1" × 12" × 18" for the sides (2)

B. 1" × 12" × 6 ¾" (1)

C. 1" × 12" × 9 ⁹⁄₁₆" (1)

D. 1 " × 12" × 11 ¼" for the back (1)

E. 1" × 12" × 17 ³⁄₁₆" for the bottom (1)

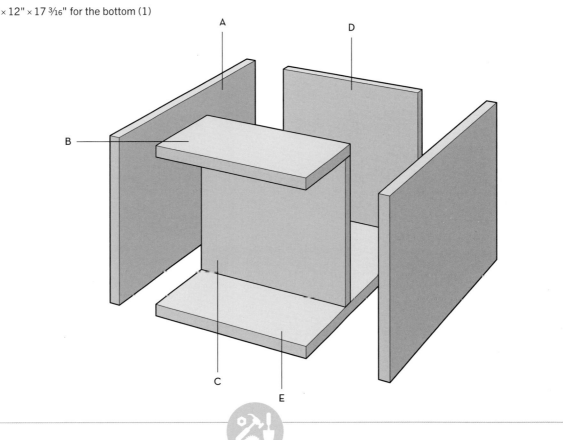

TOOLS & MATERIALS

- ☐ 1 × 12 × 8' cedar (1)
- ☐ Tape measure
- ☐ Pencil
- ☐ Particle mask, eye protection, hearing protection, work gloves
- ☐ Circular saw, miter saw, or table saw

- ☐ Drill
- ☐ ⁵⁄₁₆ × 6"-long drill bit
- ☐ Exterior wood glue
- ☐ Bar clamp
- ☐ #8 pilot/countersink bit
- ☐ #8 × 2" wood screws
- ☐ Hand sander

- ☐ 100-grit sandpaper (optional)
- ☐ Assorted tree limbs, 2" to 3" in diameter
- ☐ 72" bamboo pole
- ☐ Spray-on or brush-on rubber sealant
- ☐ Wood filler (optional)

NOTE: *For brevity's sake, when instructions state "attach," the step includes the added suggestion of drilling appropriately sized pilots and countersinks before installing screws.*

Making a Bee-Friendly Planter

1. Don safety gear and measure and cut the wood into the following dimensions:
   - 1 × 12 × 18" (sides) (2)
   - 1 × 12 × 6 ¾" (1)
   - 1 × 12 × 9 9/16" (1)
   - 1 × 12 × 11 ¼" (back) (1)
   - 1 × 12 × 17 3/16" (bottom) (1)

2. Smooth all edges of the boards with sandpaper. Use glue and screws to attach the 6 ¾-inch-long piece to the 9 9/16-inch-long piece, fashioning an L shape.

3. Glue, clamp, and attach the 18-inch-long side pieces to the L piece, as shown. Note that the shorter leg of the L faces down, thereby leaving a gap of ¾-inch facing you. (From this perspective, the planter is upside down.)

4. Glue, clamp, and attach the back of the planter between the sides.

5 Glue the bottom of the planter in place so that it is recessed between the back and side pieces and rests against the longer leg of the L.

6 Attach the bottom piece into place through the sides and into the longer leg of the L below.

7 Measure the depth of the cavity at the side of the planter, then cut segments of tree limbs to this length to fill the inside of the cavity.

8 Fill the cavity with the cut limbs, and fill any spaces between them with sections of bamboo pole cut to fit. Drill $5/16$-inch-diameter holes about 5 inches deep into one end of each of the cut limbs. (These holes provide nesting spots for bees.) Apply waterproofing to the interior of the planter, and fill screw holes, if desired as described on pages 9 and 10.

Collapsible Grow Box/ Seed-Starter

STARTING SEEDS on a sunny windowsill has its place, but if you're looking to become more serious about sprouting, then a grow box should be on your "want" list. The problem is that, like holiday decorations, grow boxes are generally only needed at certain times of the year. For us, that's a couple of months in the early spring. For the other 10 months of the year, it can be shelved away. Or, in the case of this collapsible grow box, shoved under the bed and out of sight.

Made using a 34-inch under-the-bed storage container and PVC pipe and fittings, the grow box can conveniently store all your seed-starting supplies when not in use. That's because some of joints are left unglued for easy dismantling and compacting. When assembled, the container is the perfect environment for peat pots and pellet trays, since it keeps any wayward dirt and water nicely contained.

TOOLS & MATERIALS

- ☐ One plastic under-bed storage tote with lid
- ☐ Tape measure
- ☐ Marking pen
- ☐ ½" × 20' Schedule C PVC pipe
- ☐ ½" PVC tee fittings (10)
- ☐ ½" PVC 3-way elbows (8)

- ☐ Work gloves
- ☐ PVC tubing cutter
- ☐ PVC solvent glue
- ☐ Drill
- ☐ ³⁄₁₆ × 2 ½" eyebolts (2)
- ☐ Nuts to fit the eyebolts (4)
- ☐ ³⁄₁₆" drill bit

- ☐ #16 single jack chain (8')
- ☐ 1" S-hooks to fit in links of jack chain (2)
- ☐ 24"-long grow light

Making a Collapsible Grow Box/ Seed-Starter

1. Nest a PVC 3-way elbow at each of the inside corners of the bin. Starting at one of the short ends of the bin, measure the space between the elbows and add an inch for the ½ inch of pipe that will extend into the 3-way elbow sockets at each end.

2. Wearing gloves, cut two pieces of PVC pipe to this length, using a PVC tubing cutter. These pieces will form the shorter side rails of the PVC structure. Repeat steps 1 and 2, but now measure the long ends of the bin for the longer rails of the PVC structure and add 1 inch for the ends that will be seated. Cut four pieces of PVC pipe to this length (two will form the lower rails, and two will serve as upper rails for the structure.)

3. Join together two longer rails with the two short bottom rails using the 3-way elbows. Slip the assembly inside the storage tote to check fit. Trim rails to fit if necessary.

4. The short upper rails of the assembly will each be made from two shorter lengths of pipe joined with a tee-fitting. To calculate the length of each pipe, take the length of the lower rails, subtract 1 inch, and divide by 2. For example, in our box, the short lower rails are 10 inches long. Ten minus 1 equals 9; divide by 2 to get 4.5 inches. Cut four lengths of PVC pipe to whatever length you calculate. Dry-fit the four lengths into the in-line holes of two PVC tee-fittings, as shown.

5. Dry-fit the short upper pieces (with the tee fittings) to the remaining four corner elbows, then dry-fit the two remaining long rails into the elbows. Measure the length between the opposing tee fittings and add 1 inch.

6. Cut a length of PVC to this measurement and dry-fit this length to the assembly via the two tee-fittings. (This will fashion a center beam which will support the hanging grow-light.) With PVC solvent glue, glue the top pieces together, and then repeat the process for the bottom pieces.

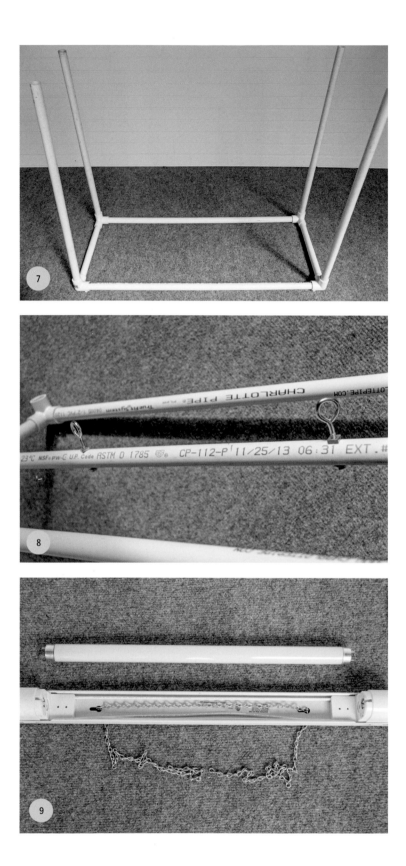

7. Cut four equal lengths of the remaining PVC to fashion the legs of the interior structure. (In our example, they are 22 ½" long.) Do not glue these in place, however, so that the structure can be disassembled.

8. Drill two holes in the top center beam spaced to match the position of the mounting holes in the grow light. Thread one nut fully on to each eyebolt, insert the bolt through the hole in the center beam, then secure it by threading the second nut onto the bolt.

9. Thread the jack chain through one of the grow-light's mounting holes and out the other, basically threading the fixture on the chain.

10. Attach S-hooks to the eyebolts. Fit the end links of the jack chain onto the S-hooks.

11. When in use, adjust the length of the chains as necessary as the seedlings sprout and grow. Nest the lid of the bin on top of the PVC structure to help reflect the light downward.

12. When not in use, the grow structure disassembles and collapses into itself, making it easy to store. This box fits the disassembled grow light frame, the grow-light, a heating mat, a timer, an extension cord, a plastic seeding tray and cover, a spray bottle (for watering tiny seedlings), extra peat pots, peat disks. and disk trays. And, yes, the container's top snaps firmly into place!

Geometric Copper Pot Sleeve

TERRCOTTA POTS are ubiquitous inhabitants of the garden and garden shed, and for good reason. They're inexpensive and dependable, and because they come in standard sizes, an 8-inch azalea pot is pretty much the same size as every other 8-inch azalea pot. That's why they're the perfect pot around which to assemble a geometric sleeve.

The particular sleeve in question is made out of ½-inch copper pipe and a collection of elbows and tees. We've chosen to paint the accompanying azalea pot white to highlight the copper and give it a more modern look, but you could also age the pot with a lime solution or even cover it in moss for a more traditional or even steampunk feel.

Assembled using polyurethane glue, the pot sleeve is quite sturdy, but for those with the equipment and expertise, soldering the sleeves joints is an option as well.

CUT LIST

½" copper pipe

- ½" × 3 ⅜" (16)
- ½" × 3 ½" (4)

TOOLS & MATERIALS

- ☐ ½" × 10' copper pipe (1)
- ☐ Eye protection, work gloves
- ☐ Copper tubing cutter
- ☐ ½" copper elbows (8)
- ☐ ½" copper tee-fittings (8)
- ☐ Polyurethane glue

- ☐ Spray bottle or sponge
- ☐ Water
- ☐ Cardboard or scrap plywood to protect your work surface
- ☐ A rubber mallet (optional)

- ☐ 8" terracotta azalea pot (a Deroma size 21 [8.3"] azalea pot was is used in this project)
- ☐ Waterproofing medium (if desired)

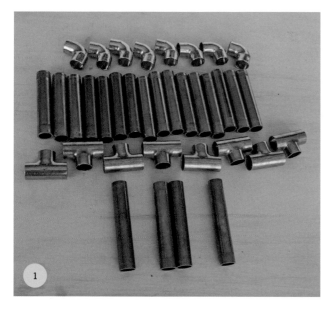

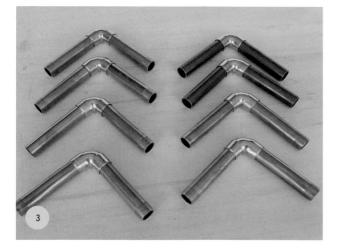

Making a Geometric Copper Pot Sleeve

1. Wearing safety gear and measure the ½-inch copper pipe into the following lengths: 16 lengths at 3 ⅜ inches and 4 lengths at 3 ½ inches.

TIP: *Before you start gluing the copper pieces together, dry fit them first as a test run.*

2. After you dismantle the assembly, glue the fittings together following the instructions on the polyurethane glue. Our glue called for pre-wetting one side of the surfaces first. (Using a spray bottle filled with water makes for quick and easy application.) To start, glue one 3 ½-inch piece of pipe into the bottom socket of each tee-fitting to create four assemblies. Push the assemblies down onto a flat surface to ensure that the tees are aligned with one another.

3. Glue one 3 ⅜-inch piece of pipe into each socket on every elbow. You'll have eight elbow assemblies when finished with this step.

4. Use glue to attach the elbow assemblies to the tee-fitting assemblies, as shown. This will take a bit of finessing in order to get the parts to fit together snugly.

4a

4b

5

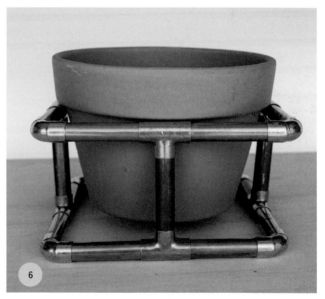

6

5   When all assemblies are glued and fit together, you may want to set the assembly on a flat surface and gently tap the parts together with a rubber mallet to tighten the joints.

6   Before the glue has fully cured, we suggest you ease the pot inside the assembly to check for fit. There should be a little ease to fit the pot, but **do not force** the pot into position, as it may pop the joints apart or damage the pot.

7   If you prefer to paint your pot, as we've done, opt to use an exterior-grade spray paint. Spray paint the pot **first**, then, after the paint is dry, tape off and cover the painted surface with newspaper and apply a waterproofing medium to the inside of the pot.

17

Infinity Planter

CUT LIST

- 1" × 8" × 16" for the
  2 sides (2)
- 1" × 8" × 14 ½" for the
  2 sides and the 2 bottom
  inserts (4)

AN *INFINITY* **POOL** is a swimming pool positioned in a way that gives the impression of merging into the ocean or landscape. Most often spotted at luxury hotels and resorts, these carefully engineered optical illusions cross over into something quite magical.

Sadly, not all of us live next to a body of water—or have the funds—to produce the effect of an infinity pool in our own backyards. There is a perfect alternative for the land-locked, however, and that is an *infinity planter*. The optical illusion has the same effect as the infinity pool, only this time it's created thanks to a bit of faux grass that blends into the lawn.

TOOLS & MATERIALS

- ☐ 1 × 8 × 8' pressure-treated
  lumber or cedar
- ☐ Tape measure
- ☐ Pencil
- ☐ Particle mask, eye protection,
  hearing protection, work gloves
- ☐ Circular saw, miter saw,
  or table saw
- ☐ Bar clamps
- ☐ Exterior glue
- ☐ Drill

- ☐ #8 pilot/countersink bit
- ☐ #8 × 2" triple-coated screws
- ☐ ½" drill bit
- ☐ Spray-on rubber or rubberized
  roof sealant
- ☐ Putty knife
- ☐ 1 × 2 × 6' mahogany lumber
- ☐ Hammer or pneumatic finish
  nailer
- ☐ 2" finish nails
- ☐ Sander

- ☐ 120-grit sandpaper
- ☐ Exterior wood stain
- ☐ Application bristle of foam
  brush
- ☐ 1' × 6' piece of faux grass carpet
- ☐ Straightedge or framing square
- ☐ Carpet knife or utility knife
- ☐ Tack hammer or pneumatic
  stapler
- ☐ ½" carpet tacks or ½" staples

Making an Infinity Planter

 Don safety gear and from the 1 × 8, cut two side pieces 16 inches long, and four pieces 14 ½ inches long for two long sides and two bottom inserts.

(2) Glue, clamp, and use 2" screws to attach together the 16-inch side boards flush to the ends of the 14 ½-inch side boards. Three screws per side will do.

(3) Dry fit one of the bottom inserts into place and trim to fit material size if necessary. When the fit is acceptable, clamp it in place and attach it with three screws. Repeat using the second bottom insert.

NOTE: *For brevity's sake, when instructions state "attach," the step includes the added suggestion of drilling appropriately sized pilots and countersinks before installing screws.*

4 Drill four ½-inch holes through the bottom of the box for drainage. Coat the interior of the box generously with spray-on rubber or rubberized roofing sealant applied with a putty knife.

5 When the sealant is dry to the touch, begin applying the mahogany trim. First, miter one end of the board at 45 degrees. Then fit the piece on the top of the box so the inside corner of the box aligns with the inside corner of the miter. **Mark the opposite-inside corner and cut the miter on that mark.** Glue and nail the piece into place. Repeat this step for the remaining three trim pieces, aligning the miters as you go.

TIP: *When inserting tight-fitting boards into place, try tapping them with a rubber mallet to get precise joints.*

5b

6

7a

7b

6. Sand the mahogany edging, if necessary, and then stain it with a high-quality exterior stain.

7. Verify the width of the box below the mahogany trim and cut a piece of faux grass to this measurement using a straightedge and a carpet knife or utility knife, and a scrap piece of plywood as a cutting board.

8. Using a tack hammer and tacks or a pneumatic stapler and staples, attach the grass, making sure the grass's backing is flush to the underside of the mahogany trim. Since most of your tacks or staples will run along the edges of the faux grass, make sure to avoid the screws at the edges of the box.

9. Use the scrap plywood to support the faux grass as you cut it to length to meet the initial installation point. Tack or staple the end securely into place.

TIP: *If fitting more than one strip of grass around the planter, make note of the grass's "nap," as each piece should match in its direction.*

18

Kids' Raised Planter/ Salad Bar

THE RAISED PLANTER featured here was designed to accompany the kids' potting bench featured on page 60. Although conceived as a set, each project also functions just fine on its own. The planter, like the potting bench, is appropriately sized for the young gardener, but its dimensions also make it great for growing lettuce. And because it's raised, it's easily tended to and is out of reach of smaller marauding garden pests. Its small footprint also means it can be kept on a patio, deck, or balcony to be used as a kitchen herb garden. Other alternatives include using it as a succulent garden or even a miniature or fairy garden.

Any naturally weather-resistant lumber will work for this project, but avoid pressure-treated lumber, as the chemicals in the wood are not advised for any project that will be used to grow food. We have used cedar for this project, which is a standard for outdoor building projects.

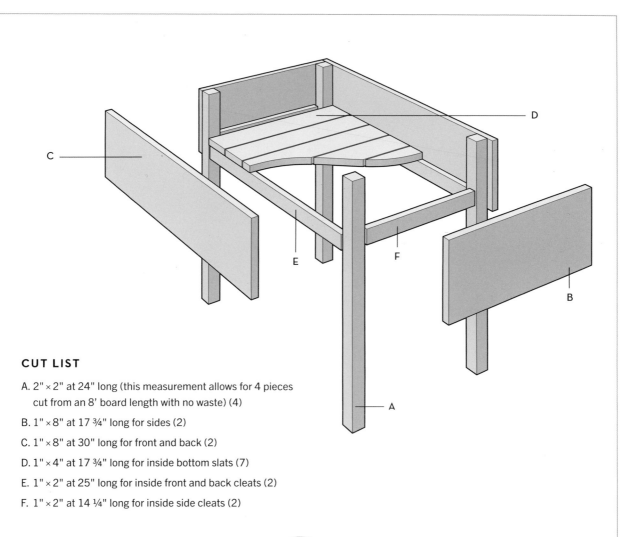

CUT LIST

A. 2" × 2" at 24" long (this measurement allows for 4 pieces cut from an 8' board length with no waste) (4)

B. 1" × 8" at 17 ¾" long for sides (2)

C. 1" × 8" at 30" long for front and back (2)

D. 1" × 4" at 17 ¾" long for inside bottom slats (7)

E. 1" × 2" at 25" long for inside front and back cleats (2)

F. 1" × 2" at 14 ¼" long for inside side cleats (2)

TOOLS & MATERIALS

- ☐ 1 × 2 × 8' cedar (1)
- ☐ 1 × 4 × 4' cedar (1)
- ☐ 1 × 8 × 8' cedar (1)
- ☐ 2 × 2 × 8' cedar (1)
- ☐ Tape measure
- ☐ Pencil
- ☐ Particle mask, eye protection, hearing protection, work gloves

- ☐ Circular saw, miter saw, or table saw
- ☐ Sander
- ☐ 80- and 100-grit sandpaper
- ☐ Two 24" bar clamps (optional)
- ☐ Exterior wood glue
- ☐ Drill
- ☐ #8 pilot/countersink bit

- ☐ #8 × 1¼" triple-coated deck screws
- ☐ #8 × 2" triple-coated deck screws
- ☐ Epoxy wood filler (optional)
- ☐ Newspaper or cocoa mat
- ☐ Scissors, if necessary

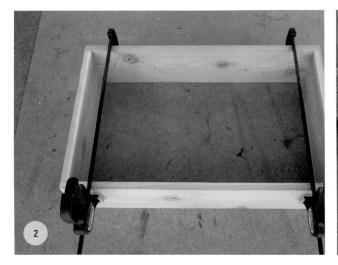

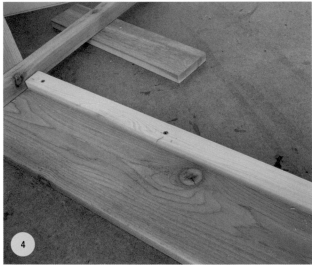

Making a Kids' Raised Planter

 Wearing safety gear, saw the boards into the following quantities and lengths:

- 2 × 2 × 24" (legs) (4)
- 1 × 8 × 17 ¾" (sides) (2)
- 1 × 8 × 30" (front and back) (2)
- 1 × 4 × 17 ¾" (inside bottom slats) (7)
- 1 × 2 × 25" (inside front and back cleats) (2)
- 1 × 2 × 14 ¼" (inside side cleats) (2)

2 Glue and clamp the two 30-inch long front and back pieces to the two 17 ¾-inch sides of the planter. Attach the front and back to the sides with 2" screws.

✏️

NOTE: *For brevity's sake, when instructions state "attach," the step includes the added suggestion of drilling appropriately sized pilots and countersinks before installing screws.*

3 Designate one side of the planter to be the top, then flip the planter over. Position one of the four 2 × 2 legs at one of the corners of the planter so that 17 ½ inches of the leg is protruding out of the bottom of the planter. Clamp the leg into place and then attach it using 2" screws. Repeat for the remaining three legs.

4 Glue and attach one of the longer cleats to the inside front bottom edge of the planter using 1 ¼" screws. Repeat for the second longer cleat.

5 Place a scrap 1 × 4 at the bottom edge of the box as a spacer to position the shorter side cleat. Attach the cleat with 1 ¼" screws. Repeat for the short cleat on the other side of the planter.

6 Position the seven slats inside the planter so they span the longer cleats with uniform spaces between boards. (You may need to adjust the slats' length if not using boards with nominal sizes.) Attach the slats with 1 ¼" screws driven down into the cleats, if desired. Cut newspaper or cocoa mat to line the bottom of the planter before planting.

Raised Miniature Garden/ Serving Side Table

YOU DON'T HAVE TO LOVE miniature gardens to love this project. That's because it can function just as easily as a serving side table. The secret to the build's versatility is the planter or serving tray portion of the structure, which is what big box stores refer to as a "utility pan." Such pans are the perfect size to use as a shallow planter or a convenient way to serve bottled or canned drinks on ice. The pans are made out of galvanized steel in such a way that they have no seams, which means they won't rust or leak.

If you opt to use the project as a miniature garden and plan to place the garden outside in the elements, you'll probably want to drill a few drainage holes in the bottom of the pan. However, if the garden will be kept under an eave, on a porch, or even inside the house, skip the holes and opt for adding gravel to the bottom of the pan to act as drainage.

Oftentimes used for DIY oil changes as catch pans, utility bins can usually be found in the automotive aisle of your local big box store or even in your nearby auto parts supply store.

This project is a simple construction featuring four legs and two X-shaped cross braces. The only moderately difficult part of the construction is the half-lap joints where the braces cross. This task will be easiest using a table saw, but it can also be done with a circular saw.

CUT LIST

- 2" × 2" × 24" for legs (4)
- 2" × 2" × ⅛" less the diameter of the pan at its largest point (4) (for cross braces)

TOOLS & MATERIALS

- ☐ 2 × 2 × 8' pressure-treated or cedar lumber (2)
- ☐ Tape measure
- ☐ Framing square
- ☐ Pencil
- ☐ Particle mask, eye protection, hearing protection, work gloves
- ☐ Circular saw or table saw
- ☐ Drill
- ☐ Hammer
- ☐ Chisel

- ☐ Exterior wood glue
- ☐ Bar clamp
- ☐ #8 pilot countersink bit
- ☐ #8 × 1¼" triple-coated deck screws
- ☐ #10 pilot/countersink bit
- ☐ #9 × 3" triple-coated deck screws
- ☐ 3-gallon utility pan (a Behrens utility pan measuring 4 × 16 inches was used in this project.)

Making a Raised Miniature Garden/ Serving Side Table

1. Don safety gear and cut four 24-inch-long pieces from the 2 × 2 to serve as legs for the garden/table. Now cut four additional 2 × 2 pieces to a length that is ⅛ inch longer than the diameter of the pan at its largest point. These will serve as the cross braces.

2. Cut 4 pieces of the 2 × 2 stock ⅛ inch longer than the diameter of the pan at its largest point. For this project, that is at the rim. The diameter at that point measures 16 ½ inches. To determine the location of the half lap joint used to put the legs' cross braces together, we'll need to do a little math and use the following formulas:

   The diameter measurement obtained in step 2—the thickness of the boards used = x

   (For example, the material thickness of the 2 × 2 used for the garden/table pictured here is 1 1/2 inches, so the formula to solve for x is: 16 1/2 inches [the measurement from step 2]– 1 1/2 inches which = 15 inches)

   Then x/2 = the edge of where the half-lap begins and ends.

   (Or, to continue with the example, 15 inches / 2 = 7 ½ inches.

   Align and clamp together all 4 pieces that will be used as cross braces (the boards cut in step 2.) Measure 7 ½ inches in from both ends of the cross braces and draw a line at each location.

3. Set the saw blade to one-half the material thickness (in our example, this means ¾ inch), and make multiple cuts inside the marked out area. These will serve as the cross brace joint.

4. Use a hammer and chisel to break off and clean up the remaining material inside the cuts.

TIP: *Clamp two of the pieces together to make the job of cutting the half-lap cuts faster and easier.*

5 Join two of the boards at their half lap joints, creating an *X*, and check for flush. If you've plunged a bit too deep with the saw, simply add a shim to the cross-section.

6 Glue and screw the *X* together—along with both sides of the shim, if you're using one—at the center of the half lap, and attach with a 1 ¼" screw. Repeat this process to make the second cross brace.

7 Measure the depth of the pan. Use this measurement to mark in from each end of each of the legs and draw a line.

8 Using glue and a bar clamp, position two opposing legs around the cross brace assemblies at the marks you have just drawn. Attach the legs to the braces with 3" screws.

9 Turn the garden/table right side up and repeat to attach the remaining two legs to the cross braces.

10 Nestle the utility pan on the upper cross braces. Fill it with ice and bottled drinks or fairy garden paraphernalia, as desired.

TIP: *Positioning the garden/table on its side and using scrap lumber to lift the assembly will make clamping and attachment much easier.*

5a

5b

6a

6b

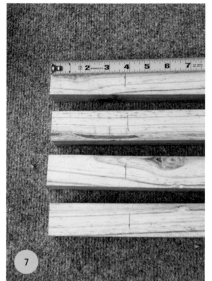

20

Terraced Tub Planter

WOODEN TUB PLANTERS come in many sizes, and just about any of them can be converted into a terraced planter. There are, however, two required elements you should look for when buying a tub to terrace. First, the tub's staves (the vertical boards themselves) shouldn't be permanently joined; instead, they should be simply fitted together with loose tongue-and-groove joints. Second, the tub should be secured with two metal bands—one higher on the tub and one lower.

Although the cedar tub in this example had nine total staves, yours may have more or even less, which means you might have to do more or less cutting. Whatever the number, trimming down half the staves—or one less than half of them—will produce the desired effect. Although tub size and stave count are flexible, material size is less so; therefore, when choosing a tub to terrace, opt for one with staves at least ⅞-inch thick.

TOOLS & MATERIALS

- ☐ 15 × 15 × 12" wood-stave tub planter
- ☐ Aviation snips or tin snips
- ☐ 1 × 6 scrap wood, about 18" long, preferably of the same wood species as the tub itself
- ☐ Particle mask, eye protection, hearing protection, work gloves

- ☐ Circular saw
- ☐ Drill
- ☐ Scrap wood
- ☐ Fine-toothed hand saw
- ☐ Wood chisel
- ☐ Hammer
- ☐ ½" round-headed zinc wood screws

- ☐ Pencil
- ☐ Marking pen
- ☐ 1 ½" round-headed zinc wood screws
- ☐ 80-grit sandpaper

Making a Terraced Tub Planter

1. Don safety gear and drill a pilot hole into the band near one of the stave's tongue-and-groove edges and fix the band in place with a ½" wood screw. Using a hammer and chisel, remove enough material below the band to the right of the screw to allow access for aviation or tin snips.

2. Using snips, cut through the upper band of the tub about ⅜ inch away from the tongue and groove. Slightly bend the excess band so it's out of the way.

3. Measure down from the top edge of the tub a distance equal to the width of the 1 × 6 (usually this will be about 5½ inches) and mark a horizontal line across approximately half of the tub's staves. (The tub used in this project had nine staves, so we marked four for removal.)

4. Using scrap wood, prop up the bottom of the tub to get it as horizontal as possible, and, using a circular saw, cut along the mark made in the last step, stopping just short of the first unmarked staves at either side of the mark drawn.

5. Use a fine-toothed hand saw to finish the cut to the ends of the marked line. Remove the cut portions of the staves.

6. Sighting down the edge of the two intact staves, use a hammer and chisel to remove their tongue and groove joinery down to the cut, squaring off the edges.

7. Pull the unattached side of the upper banding taut. Mark the band where it meets the edge of the exposed stave, and make a second mark ⅜ inch past this mark.

8. Drill a pilot hole and use a ½" wood screw to secure the band to the stave, matching the position of the screw on the opposite side. Cut this side of the band at the second mark made in step 7.

9. With the hammer, bend the ends of the banding flat against the edges of the staves.

10. Drill pilot holes into the segment of metal band you removed, then use it to support the cut staves by attaching it inside the tub with ½" wood screws.

11. Position the 1 × 6 board upright in the cutout area so it is flush against the edges of the staves. Using a pencil, mark the contour of the staves on the back of the 1 × 6. Cut at the mark made with a circular saw or fine-toothed handsaw.

12. Test fit the 1 × 6 against the exposed staves and mark the remaining "dog ear" contour of the stave. Using the fine-toothed hand saw, saw the board at the contour lines. Sand the cut edges of the staves and 1 × 6 lightly to smooth them.

13. Attach the 1 × 6 to the exposed ends of the two exposed staves by drilling pilot holes, then driving in 1 ½" wood screws. (Two screws per side will be sufficient.) All that's left is adding soil and plants.

21

Threaded Plant Hanger

PART WOODWORKING AND PART EMBROIDERY, this threaded rope plant hanger will be an attractive accent to whatever plant inhabits it. It's sized generously enough to hold a standard 8-inch terracotta pot, but be aware that a terracotta pot will add significant weight to the planter—especially after a good soaking with water. A better choice is an inexpensive (and much lighter) 8-inch plastic pot.

Although you may be tempted to plant directly into the hanger itself, it's not advised, as the holes will fill with dirt and will soon turn your lovely planter into a drippy, muddy mess. Hung from a soffit overhang, beam, or even a robust tree limb or shepherd's hook, this planter is sure to enhance any outdoor space.

CUT LIST

A. 1" × 10" × 9 ¼" for front, back, and bottom (3)

B. 1" × 10" × 10 ¾" for sides (2)

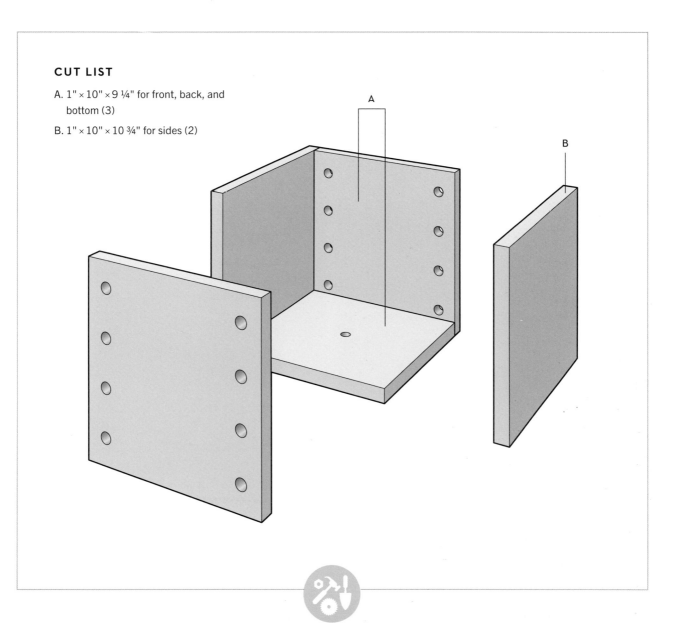

TOOLS & MATERIALS

- ☐ 1 × 10 × 8' cedar
- ☐ Tape measure
- ☐ Pencil
- ☐ Particle mask, eye protection, hearing protection, work gloves
- ☐ Circular saw or table saw
- ☐ Drill

- ☐ ⅜" and ½" drill bits
- ☐ Hand sander and 100-grit sandpaper, if desired
- ☐ Exterior glue
- ☐ 2" finish nails
- ☐ Hammer

- ☐ ½" twisted white nylon rope (20')
- ☐ Masking tape
- ☐ Scissors
- ☐ 8" plastic pot (and saucer, if using indoors)

2a

2b

3a

3b

Making a Threaded Plant Hanger

1 Don safety gear and measure, mark, and cut three 9¼-inch-long pieces from the 1×10. These will form the front, back, and bottom of planter. Cut two 10¾-inch-long pieces from the 1×10. These will fashion the sides of the planter.

2 With the wood grain running horizontally, and starting at 1¼ inches from the bottom edge and 1½ inches in from the sides, mark and drill four ³⁄₈-inch holes 2¼ inches apart along two opposing sides of the 9¼-inch tall boards.

3 Apply glue to the two opposing edges of the bottom piece, then nail the front and back to the bottom of the planter using finish nails.

4 Now apply glue to the exposed side edges of the front, back, and bottom boards, then position the 10¾-inch side boards and attach them with finish nails, completing the box. Let the glue cure as per manufacturer's instructions.

5 Drill a drainage hole at the bottom center of the planter with the ½" drill bit. Sand all boards with 100-grit sandpaper, if desired.

Lacing up the Threaded Plant Hanger

1. Wrap the center of the 20-foot-length of nylon rope with masking tape and cut the rope at the masking tape into two lengths of 10 feet each. Knot the opposite end of each length of rope.

2. Position the planter on its side. Starting at the lowest left hole facing you, thread one of the ropes up through the inside of the planter through the hole until the knot is flush against the inside of the planter. Now carry the rope over to the right lower hole and thread it down from the outside to the inside of the planter.

3. Skip the next hole on the same the side, and feed the rope up through the following hole from the inside to the outside of the planter. Carry the rope over to the opposing hole, and feed it down through that hole from outside to in. Drop this piece of rope.

4. Now repeat these steps, but start by feeding the second piece of rope up through the second hole on the bottom right of the planter. Cross over to the opposite hole, then feed the rope down into the box then up to the top holes. Finish up with the second row of holes, and when the end of the rope goes into the final hole, knot it securely from the inside.

5. Repeat steps 2 to 4 with the opposite side of the planter and the other length of rope. Make sure to follow the same lacing pattern to ensure that the rope loops are the same length when finished.

6. Hang the planter on a hook and check for balance; adjust the length of the ropes inside by forming a new knot, if necessary.

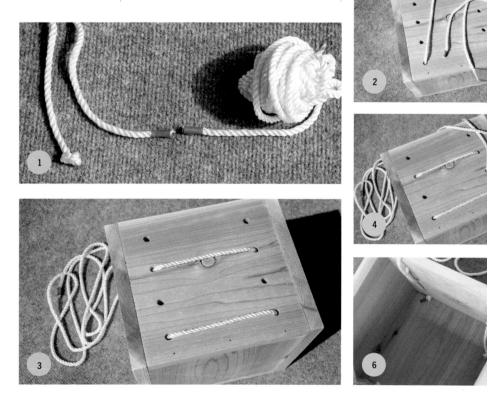

Cabinet Greenhouse

TRADITIONALLY, a greenhouse is a building, not a cabinet, but then again, most greenhouses can't fit on a deck, porch, or patio either. That's one advantage that makes this cabinet version a great addition to any gardener's collection of must-haves. Like any greenhouse, this space-saving version will extend the growing season, and it can also serve as the perfect outdoor vacation spot for your indoor houseplants during more balmy temperatures.

Although the cabinet greenhouse is a snap to build, it does require a little math. (That's because lumber material may vary in thickness and not exactly match the expected actual dimensions. But don't worry: these instructions come with a handy formula when it comes time to make the doors, so no matter what you choose for lumber, you'll have the right measurements.

Note: when filled, the cabinet is heavy and quite stable, but anchoring it to a wall is still a good precautionary measure, especially with young children about.

Like some of the projects in this book, we've built the cabinet greenhouse from cedar. You could also choose to build yours from pressure-treated lumber.

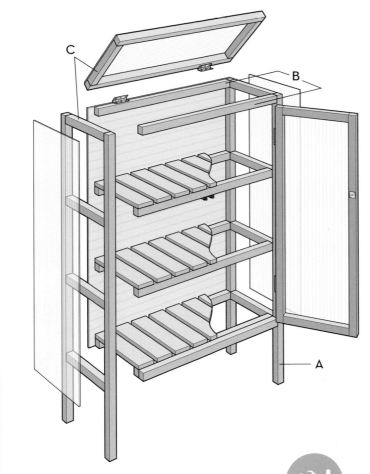

CUT LIST

A. 2" × 2" × 59" for the legs of the greenhouse (4)

B. 2" × 2" × 33 ¾" for the front and back stretchers (9)

C. 2" × 2" × 13 ½" for the side stretchers and short sides of top door (10)

TOOLS & MATERIALS

- ☐ 2 × 2 × 8' cedar (14)
- ☐ 1 × 4 × 10' cedar (3)
- ☐ Tape measure
- ☐ Pencil
- ☐ Particle mask, eye protection, hearing protection, work gloves
- ☐ Circular saw or table saw
- ☐ Miter saw
- ☐ Drill
- ☐ #10 pilot/countersink bit

- ☐ #9 × 3" triple-coated deck screws
- ☐ Bar clamps
- ☐ ⅜" × 4' × 4' sheet of exterior grade plywood
- ☐ Outdoor stain or sealant
- ☐ Application bristle or foam brush
- ☐ #8 pilot/countersink bit
- ☐ #8 × 1¼" triple-coated deck screws

- ☐ 4 × 8' clear sheet double-wall polycarbonate
- ☐ U-channel or sealing tape for the open ends of the polycarbonate
- ☐ Screws for the polycarbonate, as recommended by the manufacturer
- ☐ 3" hinges (6)
- ☐ Spring-loaded, double magnetic touch latch

Making the Cabinet Greenhouse

① Don safety gear and cut the 2 × 2 into the following lengths to build the frame of the greenhouse:

- 2 × 2 × 59" (legs) (4)
- 2 × 2 × 33 ¾" (front and back stretchers) (9)
- 2 × 2 × 13 ½" (side stretchers and short side of top door) (10)

② Assemble the back of the cabinet first. Position four of the 33 ¾-inch stretchers between two 59 inch legs at 13 ½ inches, 28 ½ inches, and 43 ½ inches from the bottom, and one flush to the tops of the legs. Attach the legs to the stretchers with 3" screws.

③ To assemble the front of the cabinet, use 3" screws to attach two of the 33 ¾-inch stretchers between the remaining two legs; one flush with the top of the legs and one at 13 ½ inches from the bottom.

④ Using 3" screws, clamp and attach eight of the 13 ½-inch side stretchers into place, matching the position of the front and back stretchers, avoiding previously installed screws in the front and back stretchers.

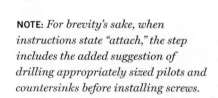

NOTE: *For brevity's sake, when instructions state "attach," the step includes the added suggestion of drilling appropriately sized pilots and countersinks before installing screws.*

5. Verify the length and width of the back of the frame. Cut the plywood siding to a size ¼ inch less than these dimensions.

6. Coat the siding with outdoor stain or sealant to protect the plywood. You can stain both sides at the same time, or, as we did, stain the decorative side now and then the outside face after installation

7. Attach the plywood to the back of the frame using 1¼" screws, decorative side facing the interior of the greenhouse, leaving a ⅛-inch gap around the entire cut sheet of plywood. Check the frame's diagonal measurements as explained on page 8 periodically to ensure the cabinet is square as you screw. Screw through the plywood back and into the inside back stretchers as well as the two back legs.

8 Attach the remaining three front stringers in place just behind the front legs and flush with the side stringers, using 3" screws.

9 To make the top door, measure the overall width of the cabinet frame and cut two 2 × 2s at this length. With 3" screws, attach these two lengths flush to the ends of the remaining two 13 ½ inch lengths cut in step one.

10 To calculate the measurement for the cabinet's two front doors' rails, use the following formula:

33 ¾ inches minus (4 × material thickness of the 2 × 2s used), minus ¾ inch (to accommodate the gap around the doors), divided by 2.

(For example, the material thickness of the 2 × 2 we used was 1⁵⁄₁₆ inches, so our formula was 33 ¾ inches minus 5 ¼ inches [or 4 times the material thickness], minus ¾ inches divided by 2 equals 13 ⁷⁄₈ inches.)

Cut four lengths of 2 × 2 to this length. (For us, that meant cutting the 2 × 2 into four pieces measuring 13 ⁷⁄₈ inches long.). These will form the horizontal rails for the front cabinet doors.

11 To calculate the cut measurement for the front doors' vertical stiles, use the following formula:

The interior vertical measurement of the front opening minus ½ inch equals your vertical measurement.

12 Construct the frame for each front door, attach two longer 2 × 2s (the stiles) with two shorter 2 × 2s (the rails) using 3" screws driven through countersunk pilot holes. The vertical stiles should overlap the ends of the horizontal rails.

13 Install all three doors (one top and two front doors) to the frame with utility hinges (two per door) using the hinges' mounting hardware and instructions

14 To make the cabinet's interior shelves, measure from the plywood back to the front edge of the front stretchers. Cut eight lengths of 1 × 4 for each shelf desired.

15 Evenly space and, using 1 ¼" screws, attach the cabinet's interior shelves to the front and back stretchers of the cabinet. (There will be approximately ½-inch gaps between each shelf board and side stretchers. One screw in the front center edge and one in the back center edge of each board will suffice.)

TIP: *When installing the two front doors, use shims to center them inside the cabinet's opening.*

16 Following the cutting procedure recommended by the manufacturer, cut the polycarbonate into three equal strips of approximately 16 inches.

TIP: *The manufacture of the polycarbonate will have designated one side with a sticker to identify it as having UV protection. This side must face **outward** when installing the polycarbonate to the cabinet. Therefore, use a bit of painter's tape to label the individual sections cut from the larger piece of polycarbonate, as they may get parted from the UV identifier.*

17 Cut the polycarbonate strips to length based upon the lengths of the front and top doors, and the sides of the cabinet. Using the manufacturer's recommended screws, attach all five pieces of polycarbonate to the cabinet, making sure the UV-protected sides are facing **outward**.

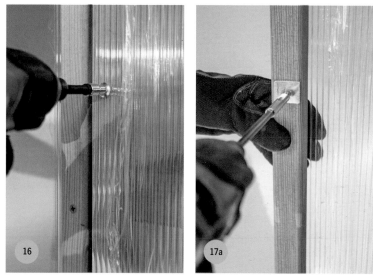

18 Finally, install the spring-loaded, double magnetic touch latch at the center of the cabinet, using its accompanying hardware and mounting instructions. To prop the top door open, you may opt to install a friction hinge, or simply cut a scrap piece of wood to prop the door open for ventilation.

Concrete & Wood Bench

ALTHOUGH THE STRAIGHT LINES of this concrete and wood bench share little with the twisted limbs of a tree, they do have one thing in common: quiet strength. Perhaps that's why they seem to go so well together.

Zen-like in its simplicity, the bench is grounded by two reinforced concrete legs weighing about 150 pounds each. As for the wood seat, it's fastened to the legs via four ⅜ × 5-inch J bolts, so it's not going anywhere either. Is the bench heavy? Absolutely—but that also means it's virtually impervious to the most robust of winds. To make installing the bench easier, it is made in parts, which can be moved to the desired location and then assembled.

CUT LIST

Wood

A. 2" × 4" × 15" for the sides and center crossmembers of the seat deck frame (3)

B. 2" × 4" × 42 ½" for the front and back of the seat deck frame (2)

C. 2" × 4" × 48" for the seat bed (5)

D. 4" × 6" × 18" for the bench's arms (2)

For Concrete Form

• 2" × 4" × 18" for arm relief (1)

½" Plywood

• ½" × 18" × 18" for bottom of form (1)

• ½" × 6" × 18" for sides of form (2)

• ½" × 6" × 19" for sides of form (2)

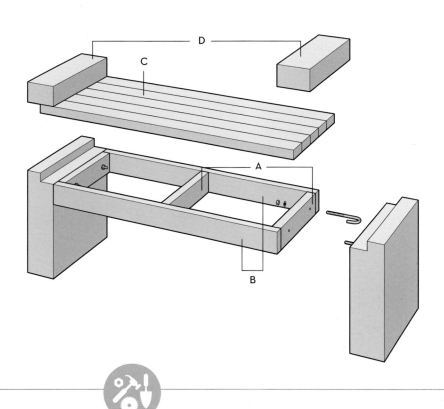

TOOLS & MATERIALS

☐ 2 × 4 × 8' pressure-treated lumber (5)
☐ 4 × 6 × 8" pressure-treated lumber (1)
☐ ½" × 2' × 4' plywood
☐ Tape measure
☐ Pencil
☐ Particle mask, eye protection, hearing protection, work gloves, latex or rubber gloves
☐ Circular saw, miter saw, or table saw
☐ Drill

☐ #10 pilot/countersink bit
☐ #8 pilot/countersink bit
☐ #9 × 3" triple-coated deck screws
☐ #8 × 1 ¼" wood screws
☐ Wheelbarrow or 5-gallon mixing pail
☐ 80-pound bags of crack-resistant, reinforced concrete (4)
☐ Shovel, paddle or mixing stick for mixing concrete
☐ Water

☐ ⅜" × 5" J-bolts with nuts and washers (4)
☐ Scrap piece of 4 × 4 to use as tamper
☐ Scrap 2 × 4 boards to use as spacers
☐ 6" or larger putty knife
☐ Portland cement (optional)
☐ Silica sand (optional)
☐ ⁷⁄₁₆" drill bit
☐ Adjustable wrench or pliers

Making a Concrete & Wood Bench

1 Don safety gear and cut the lumber into the following quantities and lengths for the wood seat:

- 2 × 4 × 15" (sides and center crossmembers of the seat deck frame) (3)
- 2 × 4 × 42 ½" (front and back of the seat deck frame) (2)
- 2 × 4 × 48" (seat bed) (5)
- 4 × 6 × 18" (bench arms) (2)

2 Cut the lumber and plywood into the following sizes to construct the concrete leg form:

- 2 × 4 × 18" (arm relief) (1)
- ½" × 18" × 18" (bottom of form) (1)
- ½" × 6" × 18" (sides of form) (2)
- ½" × 6" × 19" (sides of form) (2)

NOTE: *For brevity's sake, when instructions state "attach," the step includes the added suggestion of drilling appropriately sized pilots and countersinks before installing screws.*

3 Starting with the seat deck frame, and using the 3" screws, attach two of the 2 × 4 × 15" crossmembers flush with the sides of one of the 42 ½-inch boards and one 15-inch centered on the 42 ½-inch board.

4 Using 3" screws, attach the second 42 ½-inch board into place flush with the ends of the 15-inch crossmembers installed in the last step.

5 Position the five 48-inch seat bed boards on top of the deck frame so that 2 ¾ inches of the boards overhang on each side of the deck frame below. Using 3" screws, attach the seat bed boards to the frame at each of the three crossmembers below.

6. Begin building the cast form for the legs by positioning the two 19-inch side pieces and the 18-inch side pieces around the 18 × 18-inch bottom piece. Screw all the pieces together with 1¼" screws.

7. With 1¼" screws, attach the wide side of the 2 × 4 × 18-inch arm relief to one of the box's interior walls, 2 ¾ inches up from the bottom interior of the box.

TIP: *Cut two 2 ¾-inch scrap pieces of 2 × 4 to use as spacers to set the height of the arm relief, but remember to remove them before you pour concrete.*

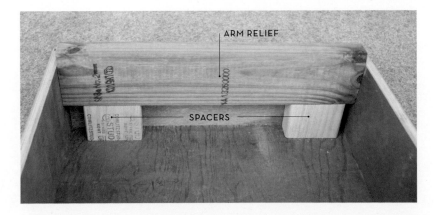

8 Erring on the side of looser (wetter) mix will help fill the form more evenly. Fill the form with concrete, starting with the cavity under the 2 × 4 arm relief. A scrap piece of 4 × 4 can help pack the concrete firmly into the form.

9 When the form is completely full, and the concrete is still wet, smooth off the top with a putty knife and insert the two J bolts 1¾ inches down from the bottom of the 2 × 4 arm relief and about 4 inches in from each side of the box. At this point, 2- to 2½ inches of the J-bolts' threads should be protruding out of the concrete.

10 After the concrete has cured, unscrew the plywood sides and release the part. Clean the plywood mold, then reassemble it to make a second leg, repeating steps 6 to 9.

11 When the second leg has fully cured, you may opt to skim coat both legs. To do this, mix 1 part Portland cement with 2 parts silica sand. The ideal consistency is similar to store-bought cake frosting. Don a pair of rubber or latex gloves and smooth the Portland/silica mixture over the entire exposed surface of the legs, filling in any voids that might have occurred when filling the leg mold.

12 Once the skim coat has cured, mark the 15-inch sides of the seat at the position of the J bolts. Drill 7⁄16-inch holes in the sides of the seat at these points to accept the J bolts. Make sure to designate the sides as Right and Left to facilitate fitting the pieces later.

TIP: *A power hand-tool that produces a lot of vibration, such as a reciprocating saw without the blade, can help settle the concrete if you run the powered-up tool along the edge of the concrete form after filling it.*

13   It's advised to move the parts of the bench to their intended location before actually assembling them, as each leg will weigh close to 150 pounds. Once at the location, position the legs at the necessary distance for the bench seat—about 42½ inches with a few inches added to account for J-bolt threads. Also make sure the legs are level, both front-to-back and across the length of the bench.

14   Dry-fit the bench together, including setting the arms in place. Mark the arm positions, remove them, and flip the bench seat over. Position the inside edge of the 4 × 6 arms at the marks you just made. Screw the arms into place through the bottom of the seat boards, using 3" screws. (One screw for each board will suffice.)

15   Set the bench's seat onto one of its legs—noting which side is left or right—and secure to the J-bolts with washers and nuts. Coax the other leg into position, slipping it through the holes for the J-bolts. Thread the remaining two washers and nuts on the J-bolts and tighten securely with an adjustable wrench or pliers.

Firewood Rack

FOR MANY OF US, yards mean trees, and trees mean pruning, and pruning means wood—lots and lots of wood, as it seems to multiply once you start cutting those downed limbs into more manageable pieces.

If, of course, we have a wood-burning fireplace or outdoor fire pit, we can put those fallen pieces to good use. We still have to store all that wood, however, which can be daunting. Sure, we can find an empty spot in the back of the yard and stack it in a pile. But rough piles of wood eventually fall over—they always do. Plus, firewood ideally should be stored off the ground to promote air flow. Otherwise, it may rot quickly and attract bugs, making it undesirable for use in an indoor fireplace.

The firewood rack featured here, however, which includes an upper area for kindling and a lower area for split logs, solves all of those problems and more. Besides keeping the firewood tidy and off the ground, it also looks great.

CUT LIST

A. 2 × 4 × 5' (See note in step 1 of instructions as to the vagaries of board lengths.) (28)

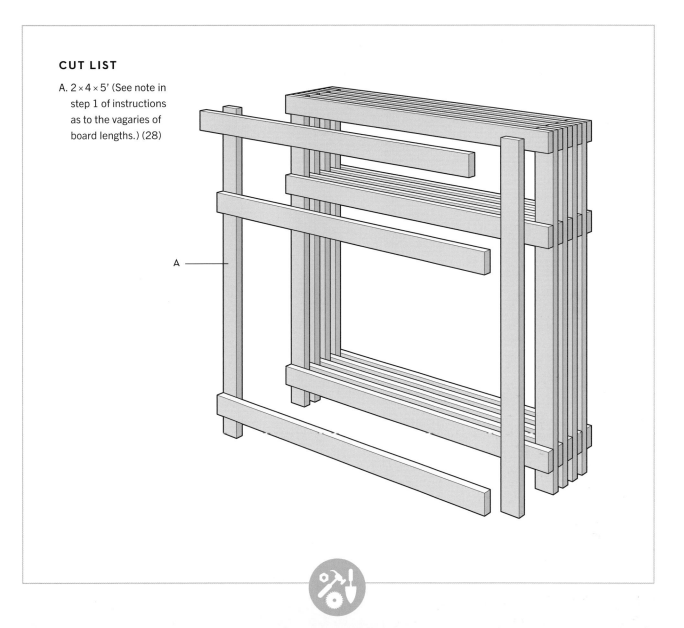

A

TOOLS & MATERIALS

- ☐ 2 × 4 × 10' pressure-treated lumber (14)
- ☐ 2 × 2 × 16" scrap pressure-treated lumber (2)
- ☐ 2 × 2 × 20" scrap pressure-treated lumber (2)
- ☐ Tape measure
- ☐ Pencil
- ☐ Particle mask, eye protection, hearing protection, work gloves
- ☐ Circular saw, miter saw, or table saw
- ☐ Drill
- ☐ #10 pilot/countersink bit
- ☐ #9 × 3" triple-coated deck screws
- ☐ #8 × 2 ½" triple-coated deck screws (optional)
- ☐ Speed square (optional)

Making a Firewood Rack

1. Don safety gear, and cut the 2 × 4s into lengths of 5 feet—or in half, as not all 10-foot boards in the bin at the lumber yard actually measure 10 feet. Lay out two 5-foot boards next to each other and mark them both at 15½ inches and 52½ inches down from the top.

2. Separate the two marked boards so they are 5 feet apart from outside to outside, keeping them parallel to each other. Measure diagonals: equal measurements means the boards are parallel.

3. Position another 5-foot-long board across the parallel boards, flush with the tops. Attach the board into place at each junction point by driving in **one** optional 2½" screw, or using **one** 3" screw angled slightly so it doesn't protrude out the back side.

NOTE: *For brevity's sake, when instructions state "attach," the step includes the added suggestion of drilling appropriately sized pilots and countersinks before installing screws.*

④ Attach the second horizontal board 52 ½ inches from the top (at the bottom marks) and flush with the sides of the vertical boards. Again, drive one screw into each junction point. Attach a third horizontal board at the 15 ½-inch mark with one screw into each junction point.

TIP: *Why only install just ONE screw at each junction point? Because that way the structure can still pivot (or 'rack'), thereby making it possible to square it up. To do this, measure from one corner to its opposite, diagonal corner. Repeat with the other two corners. If both measurements are equal, you know your structure is square. If they aren't equal, adjust at the pivot points as necessary in small increments until both measurements are equal.*

⑤ When you've determined the structure is square, screw a second screw into each of the six pivot points.

⑥ Flip the structure over. At this point, the backside of the structure is facing down. Attach the 16-inch scrap pieces of the 2 × 2 perpendicular to the bottom of each foot and flush with the outside edge of the vertical boards. This is a temporary stop that will help ensure the subsequent boards are installed square.

⑦ Screw the 20-inch pieces of scrap 2 × 2 to the outside of the 2 × 4 and 16-inch scrap pieces, using a speed square to make sure the pieces are square.

8

The next layer of boards, which we'll call the third layer, consists of placing three horizontal boards over the legs and matching in position the horizontals below in the first layer. After they are positioned, attach the third layer of boards into place, staggering the location of the screws so as not to collide with those in the second I layer. (Two screws at each intersection will suffice.)

TIP: *As you add layers to the rack, you may want to use a speed square to further verify their alignment.*

9. Install the next layer vertically, aligning the boards precisely with the underlying layer. Attach the boards in place with 3" screws.

10. Continue layering and installing the 2 × 4s until all are used.

11. Remove the temporary stops and diagonal braces.

12. Position the firewood rack upright in its final location. Although the rack will be quite stable, especially when loaded with firewood, it's still a good idea to secure it to a structure, especially if there is any danger of children climbing on it. A 4" screw screwed into a framing member of the structure/building should do just fine.

Gardener's Bench

AFTER A LONG DAY of gardening, it's time to admire all your hard work. Grab a cold drink and a comfy pillow or two and look for a shady spot. The only thing you're missing is this gardener's bench.

Why call it a *gardener's bench* and not simply a *garden bench*? Because it's been designed with the gardener in mind.

Although the bench is plenty sturdy, it's also lightweight, which means you can move it anywhere in the yard to take advantage of the view. Peonies blooming in the backyard? Move it there to enjoy the robust flowers and sweet scent. Clematis getting showy in the front yard? It can go there too. Or maybe it's that shady spot that's calling.

Wherever you want it, your gardener's bench is waiting for you there with a wide arm on which to set your cold drink and prop your pillows.

CUT LIST

A. 1" × 4" × 16" for seat bed frame sides and center crossmembers (4)

B. 1" × 4" × 48" for seat bed frame front and back (2)

C. 1" × 6" × 21 ½" for arms (2)

D. 1" × 6" × 48" for seat top (3)

E. 2" × 2" × 27 ¼" for legs (4)

F. 2" × 2" × 48" for center leg stretcher (1)

G. 2" × 2" × 4" for arm corbels (4)

H. 1" × 4" × 14 ½" for upper arm rail (2)

I. 2" × 4" × 14 ½" for lower arm rail (2)

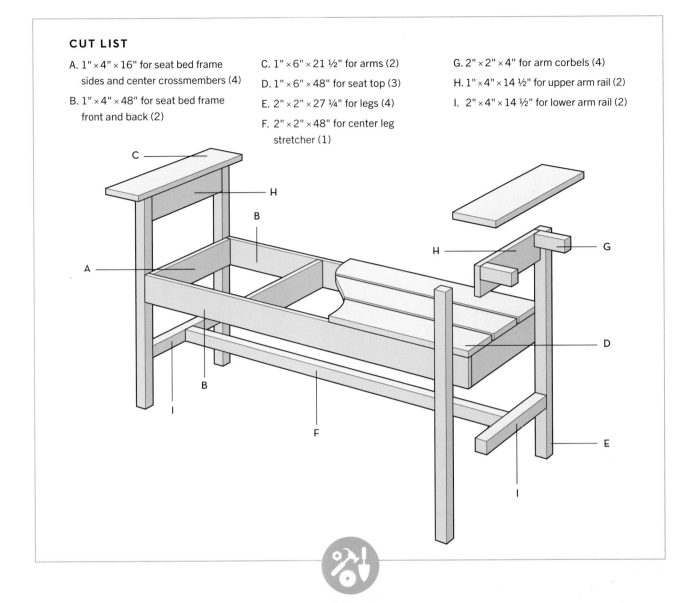

TOOLS & MATERIALS

- ☐ 1 × 4 × 8' pressure-treated lumber (2)
- ☐ 1 × 6 × 8' pressure-treated lumber (2)
- ☐ 2 × 2 × 8' pressure-treated lumber (3)
- ☐ Tape measure
- ☐ Pencil

- ☐ Particle mask, eye protection, hearing protection, work gloves
- ☐ Circular saw, miter saw, or table saw
- ☐ #8 pilot/countersink bit
- ☐ #10 pilot countersink bit
- ☐ #8 × 2" triple-coated deck screws

- ☐ #9 × 3" triple-coated deck screws
- ☐ Bar clamps
- ☐ Exterior glue
- ☐ #8 × 1 ¼" triple-coated deckscrews

Making a Gardener's Bench

1 Don safety gear and cut the lumber into the following quantities and lengths:

- 1 × 4 × 16" (seat bed frame sides and center crossmembers) (4)
- 1 × 4 × 48" (seat bed frame front and back) (2)
- 1 × 6 × 21 ½" (arms) (2)
- 1 × 6 × 48" (seat top) (3)
- 2 × 2 × 27 ¼" (legs) (4)
- 2 × 2 × 48" (center leg stretcher) (1)
- (4) 2 × 2 × 4" (arm corbels) (4)
- 13 ¾"-long scrap wood to use as spacers (2)

2 Test-fit the seat bed frame sides flush to the ends of the seat bed front and back, and evenly space the center crossmembers between the two frame sides.

3 Clamp and glue together the seat bed front and back to the seat bed frame sides and crossmembers. Attach the individual components together with 2" screws.

4 Check to make sure that the seat bed frame is squared up by measuring diagonals described on page 8. Then, evenly space the three 1 × 6 × 48 on top of the completed seat frame, and glue and attach them into place with 2" screws.

NOTE: *For brevity's sake, when instructions state "attach," the step includes the added suggestion of drilling appropriately sized pilots and countersinks before installing screws.*

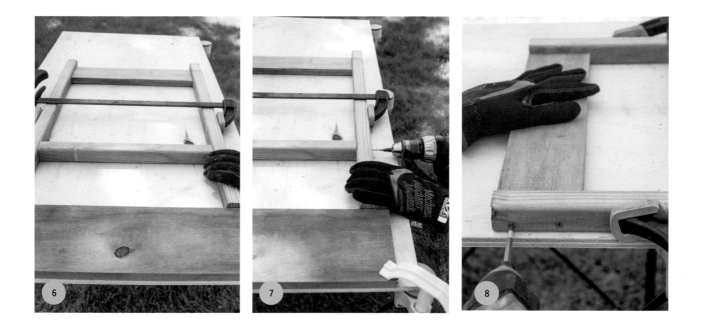

5   To determine the length of the side leg rails and arm rails, take the depth measurement of the bench's seat of 17 1/2" minus the material thicknesses of two 2 × 2 legs which will equal the length of the two parts.

For example, the material thickness of the 2 × 2 used in the bench pictured here is 1 5/16 inches, so the formula to calculate the length of the leg and arm rails is 17 1/2 inches [the depth measurement of the bench's seat] minus 2 5/8 inches [that is, 2 times 1 5/16 inches] equals 14 7/8 inches.

Cut two 2 × 2s at the number calculated for the bottom leg rails and two 1 × 4s for the upper arm rails.

6   Clamp a scrap piece of board to a work surface, then position one end of the bench legs against it. This will keep the legs square as you assemble the side of the bench. Clamp one bottom leg rail and one upper arm rail between the legs. (The lower rail should be at 6 1/8 inches from the foot of the leg, and the upper arm rail should be flush with the top and one edge of the leg).

7   Using 3" screws, attach the legs into the bottom leg rail.

8   Attach upper legs to arms with 3" screws.

Two screws per side of the upper arm brace will suffice. Repeat steps 6 to 8 to build the opposite legs-and-rail assembly.

9 With the seat assembly turned upside down, use two 13 ¾-inch spacers to align the leg assemblies with the seat assembly. Clamp the spacers and one leg assembly to the seat, orienting it so the flush side of the arm brace faces inward.

10 Using 2" screws, attach the legs to the seat assembly from inside the side seat bottom and into each leg. Two screws per joint will suffice.

11 Reinforce these joints from the outside by drilling countersunk pilot holes and driving 3" screws. Repeat steps 9 to 11 for the other leg assembly.

12 Clamp, glue, and attach the center leg stretcher to the center of the bottom leg rails with 3" screws.

13 Flip the bench right-side up and use a scrap piece of 1 × 4 as a spacer to set the overhang of the arm on the bench seat side. Center the arm so the overhang is equal on the front and back of the bench. Using 2" screws, attach the arms to the top of the leg assemblies. One screw in the center of each 2 × 2 leg and one screw at the center of the arm rail itself will do.

14 Attach the four corbels under the arms and adjacent to the 2 × 2 legs by driving 1 ¼" screws from the side of the arm into the end of the corbel and from the top of the arm down into the long side of the corbel.

26

Pergola Awning with Integrated Lighting

A UNIQUE AND FUNCTIONAL finishing touch to a garden shed door is a pergola awning. In the daytime, it offers dappled shade while providing a visually interesting architectural element to a flat, boring wall. Solar lighting adds a feature that will usher in the nighttime as well. If you're so inclined, you can opt instead to install a small trellis at the side of the awning and encourage vines to grow across it, creating a perfect spot for showy blossoms.

This pergola awning design features rafters that extend out in all three exposed directions, creating a more symmetrical canopy construction than a typical pergola.

The awning is made in parts for easier installation, and its mood lighting is provided by simple solar handrail lights. Although the completed project is shown featured above a 5-foot-wide garden shed door, it is also perfectly suited to any door or window with a few simple adjustments to its overall dimensions.

Construction of the pergola awing involves making standard miter cuts, as well as chamfer and double miter cuts, making it slightly more advanced than other projects.

CUT LIST

A. 2" × 2" × 13 ½" mitered at one end for side purlins (2)

B. 2" × 2" × 70" mitered at one end for front purlin (1)

C. 2" × 4" × 12" for horizontal brackets (4)

D. 2" × 4" × 17" for vertical brackets (2)

E. 2" × 4" × 23 ½" chamfered at one end for rafter (4)

F. 2" × 4 × 32" chamfered at one end and double mitered on the other for corner rafter (2) F

G. 2" × 4" × 93" for ledger board chamfered at both ends (1) G

H. 4" × 4" × 18 ⅜" point to point, with miters at both ends for diagonal brackets (2) H

TOOLS & MATERIALS

- ☐ 2 × 2 × 8' pressure-treated lumber (2)
- ☐ 2 × 4 × 10' pressure-treated lumber (4)
- ☐ 4 × 4 × 4' pressure-treated lumber (1)
- ☐ Tape measure

- ☐ Pencil
- ☐ Particle mask, eye protection, hearing protection, work gloves
- ☐ Circular saw, miter saw, or table saw
- ☐ Handsaw
- ☐ Framing square

- ☐ Bar clamps
- ☐ #10 pilot/countersink bit
- ☐ #9 × 3" screws
- ☐ ¼ × 4" triple-coated construction lag screws
- ☐ Solar handrail lights (3)

Making a Pergola Awning with Integrated Lighting

NOTE: *For brevity's sake, when instructions state "attach," the step includes the added suggestion of drilling appropriately sized pilots and countersinks before installing screws.*

1. Don safety gear and cut the lumber into the following quantities and lengths:

   - 2 × 2 × 13 ½" (side purlins, mitered at one end) (2)
   - 2 × 2 × 70" (front purlin, mitered at one end) (1)
   - 2 × 4 × 12" (horizontal brackets) (4)
   - 2 × 4 × 17" (vertical brackets) (2)
   - 2 × 4 × 23 ½" (rafter, chamfered at one end) (4)
   - 2 × 4 × 32" (rafter, chamfered at one end and double mitered on the other) (2)
   - 2 × 4 × 93" (ledger board, chamfered at both ends) (1)
   - 4 × 4 × 18 ⅜" (diagonal brackets, mitered at both ends) (2)

2a

Miter:

Chamfer:

Double Miter:

EXAMPLES OF A STANDARD 45-DEGREE MITER CUT COMPARED TO THE CHAMFER AND DOUBLE MITER CUTS USED IN THIS PROJECT.

To make a chamfer cut on the 2 × 4 boards specified in this project, measure 2 ½ inches in both directions at one of the corners of the board (4 inch side facing up). Mark the points, and draw a straight line from point to point. Then simply cut at the line.

To make the double miter cuts used in this project, first find the center at the end of the board (2-inch side facing up). Then measure and mark from the end of the board ¾ inch in both directions. Draw lines at the ¾ inch marks to the center mark made earlier. Remove the excess material.

2b

3

2. Clamp two 2 × 4 × 12" horizontal bracket arms to the top of one of the 2 × 4 × 17" vertical bracket arms. Check for square and attach with two 3" screws on each side.

3. Slip one of the 4 × 4 pieces into two of the bracket arms so both miters are flush with the corresponding bracket arms; mark along the bracket arms as indicated in the accompanying photo.

4. Cut the miter off at the mark made in step 3. If using a circular saw, you will need to use a handsaw to cut through the remaining thickness of the 4 × 4.

5. Slip the mitered piece back into the bracket assembly and clamp the pieces together.

6. With 3" screws, attach the mitered piece into place between both horizontal bracket arms and into the vertical bracket arms. Repeat steps 2 to 6 for the other bracket.

7. To begin construction of the top of the pergola, lay out the rafters along the ledger board according to personal preference. Mark the ledger where each individual (shorter) rafter will be attached. Note that the corner rafter meets the other perpendicular rafter.

8 Attach each rafter to the ledger by driving 3" screws through the back of the ledger and into the rafters. Attach the upper screw first, then check for square before driving the lower screw.

9 Attach the corner rafters to the ledger with two 3" screws through the ledger and one screw through the adjacent rafter.

10 With 3" screws, attach the three mitered 2 × 2 purlins centered to the top of the rafters.

11 Attach the long purlin running perpendicular to the ledger with 3" screws driven down into the rafters below.

8a

8b

9a

9b

13a

13b

12. Using ¼ × 4"-long construction lag screws, attach the bracket assemblies to each side of the shed door opening and into a framing member of the shed itself.

13. Verify the length of the beam to span the brackets. Cut a 2 × 4 to that length (the length in the example here is 70 inches). Clamp the beam to the brackets, then attach it with ¼ × 4" construction lag screws.

14. Set and center the purlin assembly atop the bracket and beam assembly. Attach the purlin assembly to the shed by driving ¼ × 4" construction lag screws through the ledger and into a framing member of the shed.

15. Toe-screw the purlin assembly to the front of each bracket by driving a 3" screw through the corner rafter and into the bracket below.

16. Using the accompanying hardware, attach the solar railing lights to the beam. The size of our pergola awning requires a single light centered on the space between each of the front rafters.

Modular Critter-Proof Vegetable Garden

THIS MODULAR CRITTER-PROOF GARDEN is all about customization. You can make two smaller boxes for two smaller, 12-inch-high, raised beds, or stack them to make one 24-inch-high bed. Or, mix and match two or more larger boxes with two or more smaller boxes, if you have the space.

If you have garden pests such as rabbits and deer, add the optional screens and doors to make the garden virtually impervious to them. It really is all up to you, your needs, and the contours of your yard.

Note that the following instructions are for the configuration we're featuring here, which includes one larger planter, two smaller planters, six screens, and two doors.

This garden could be built with any weather-resistant lumber, though we recommend against pressure-treated lumber due to the chemicals it contains. These chemicals aren't a good idea for any structure that will grow edibles.

CUT LIST

A. 2" × 12" × 72" for sides of long planter (2)

B. 2" × 12" × 36" for the ends of long planter and 3 sides of smaller planters (8)

C. 2" × 12" × 33" for center brace of long planter and 1 side of smaller planters (3)

D. 2" × 2" × 1' for cleats (8)

If making the optional critter-proof fence

E. 2" × 2" × 36" for top and bottom of panels and upper roof bracket/brace (13)

F. 2" × 2" × 60" for sides of panels (12)

G. 2" × 2" × 59 ½ for sides of doors (4)

H. 2" × 2" × 33" for center brace of panels (6)

I. 2" × 2" × 35 ½" for top and bottom of door A (2)

J. 2" × 2" × 34 for top and bottom of door B (2)

K. 2" × 2" × 32 ½" for center of door A (1)

L. 2" × 2" × 31" for center of door B (1)

M. 2" × 2" × 71" for upper roof bracket/brace, includes extra ½" for adjustment (1)

N. 2" × 2" × 38" for upper roof bracket/brace, includes extra ½" for adjustment (1)

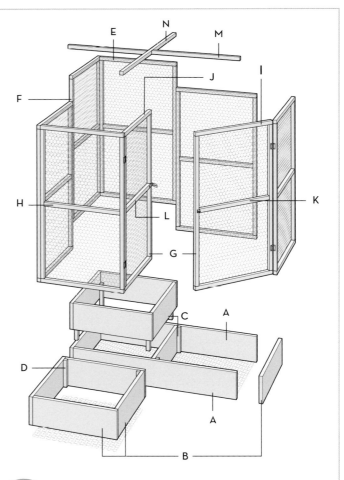

TOOLS & MATERIALS

- ☐ 2 × 12 × 10' lumber for the planter boxes (5)
- ☐ 2 × 12 × 8 lumber for the planter boxes (1)
- ☐ 2 × 2 × 8' lumber (26)
- ☐ Tape measure
- ☐ Pencil
- ☐ Particle mask, eye protection, hearing protection, work gloves
- ☐ Circular saw, miter saw, or table saw

- ☐ Drill
- ☐ #10 pilot/countersink bit
- ☐ #9 × 3" triple-coated deck screws
- ☐ #8 pilot/countersink bit (optional)
- ☐ #8 × 2 ½" triple-coated deck screws (optional)
- ☐ 3 × 50' poultry netting
- ☐ Tin snips, aviation snips, or wire cutter

- ☐ Stapler
- ☐ ½" staples
- ☐ Two bar clamps
- ☐ Wood shims
- ☐ 2" removable hinges (4)
- ☐ 3" hasp closure
- ☐ Carabiner

Making a Modular Critter-Proof Vegetable Garden

1. To make the three-tiered boxes shown in the example, don safety equipment, and measure, mark, and cut the 2 × 12 boards into the following quantities and lengths:
   - 2 × 12 × 72" (sides of long planter) (2)
   - 2 × 12 × 36" (the ends of long planter and 3 sides of smaller planters) (8)
   - 2 × 12 × 33" (center brace of long planter and 1 side of smaller planters) (3)
   - 2 × 2 × 1" (cleats) (8)

2. If making the optional pest-proof screens, mark and cut the 2 × 2 boards into the following quantities and lengths:
   - 2 × 2 × 36" (top and bottom of panels and upper roof bracket/brace) (13)
   - 2 × 2 × 60" (sides of panels) (12)
   - 2 × 2 × 59 ½" (sides of doors) (4)
   - 2 × 2 × 33" (center brace of panels) (6)
   - 2 × 2 × 35 ½" (top and bottom of door A) (2)
   - 2 × 2 × 34" (top and bottom of door B) (2)
   - 2 × 2 × 32 ½" (center of door A) (1)
   - 2 × 2 × 31" (center of door B) (1)
   - 2 × 2 × 71" (upper roof bracket/brace, includes extra ½" for adjustment) (1)
   - 2 × 2 × 38" (upper roof bracket/brace, includes extra ½" for adjustment) (1)

3. Starting with the large bottom box, attach the two 36-inch lengths flush to the ends of the 72-inch boards using 3" screws.

TIP: *Using 2 × 2" × 8' board lenghts, cut off the 36"-long pieces first and use the leftovers for the uprights, which will measure 60", less the saw blade width.*

NOTE: *For brevity's sake, when instructions state "attach," the step includes the added suggestion of drilling appropriately sized pilots and countersinks before installing screws.*

4 Attach one of the 33-inch lengths centered inside the rectangle you just made, using 3" screws.

5 Moving on to the smaller planters, take two 36-inch boards and, using 3" screws, attach them both flush to a third 36-inch board, fashioning a *U* shape with a 33-inch opening.

6 Complete the small planter box by slipping a 33-inch board inside the open end of the *U*, flush with the ends, and attach it in place with 3" screws. Repeat steps 5 and 6 to make a total of two small planters.

7 Cut poultry fence to size, and staple it onto the bottom of each planter **that will be in contact with the ground**. For example, one of the smaller planters in our project is mounted to the larger planter below so the former doesn't need the poultry fence barrier.

8 With the boxes in their permanent home, flip them over (screen side down) and position one of the smaller boxes next to the larger box so the 33-inch cut board is **next to** and **flush with** one of the ends of the larger box, creating an L shape.

TIP: *While assembling the planters, use a speed square to keep the shorter length boards perpendicular to the longer boards.*

9   Attach the smaller box to the larger with optional 2 1/2" screws or use 3" screws driven in at an angle so they don't protrude from the other side.

10 Attach the remaining small box onto the larger box using four of the 2 × 2 cleats, attaching one cleat into each corner of the smaller box using the optional 2 ½" screws or using 3" screws driven in at an angle so they don't protrude from the other side.

11 To stabilize the remaining two corners of the larger planter and the two corners of the adjacent, smaller planter, attach four 2 × 2 cleats on the inside corners, again using the optional 2 ½" screws or using 3" screws driven in at an angle so they don't protrude from the other side.

12 Now moving on to the optional panels, use 3" screws to attach two 36-inch lengths of 2 × 2 flush to the top and bottom of two 60-inch lengths. Repeat this step to make six frames.

13 Using 3" screws, attach a 33" length of 2 × 2 at the center of each frame made in the last step.

14 The doors of the garden are made exactly like the panels, except the dimensions of the board material are different. To make door A, use 3" screws to attach two 35 ½-inch lengths of 2 × 2 flush to the ends of two 59 ½-inch lengths. Then attach the 32 ½-inch length at the center of the frame just made.

15 To make door B, use 3" screws to attach two 34-inch lengths of 2 × 2 flush to the ends of two 59 ½-inch lengths, then attach the 31-inch length at the center of the frame just made.

NOTE: *The garden's design was constructed in such a way that the panels measure 36 inches wide, the same width as the poultry fence. That means each vertical side of the fencing has a factory edge that is smooth and doesn't require cutting.*

16. To install poultry fence on the panels, unroll the fence on top of the panel itself. Then staple the fence onto one side of each panel. Cut the fence 1 ½-inch longer on one end. This end will become the bottom of the panel.

17. Fold the excess 1 ½-inch of fence down and over the bottom 2 × 2. (Folding the raw fencing over at the bottom of the panel like this will further reinforce it and cover the sharp cut wire ends after the panel is installed.)

18. Install poultry fencing to the doors as you did the panels, but this time cut the fencing to length as the fence will NOT be folded under the bottom of the doors. In addition, because the doors are narrower than the fencing, you'll need to cut the width to fit. Be sure the cut edge of the fencing is attached to the hinge side of the doors and away from the point of entry.

19 When you're finished installing the fencing, it's time to install the panels to the raised beds. To do this, position them on the beds **fencing side in**. Using 3" screws, attach the bottom of the panels to the top of the boxes below—except for inside corner of the structure, as this is where the doors will be installed.

20 Clamp adjacent panels to each other and screw them together with optional 2 ½" screws. Again, if using 3" screws, simply drive the screws at an angle, but this time use an **upward** angle, as it will help prevent moisture from accumulating in the holes.

21 To assemble the upper braces, use 3" screws to attach the 36- and 38-inch boards to the 71-inch board. Install the braces to the top of the panel structure, attaching the 71-inch board opposite the door opening first. Then attach the 36-inch length to the side panel. The unattached brace ends allow you to plumb the side panels adjacent to the doors. Once side panels are plumb, clamp or temporarily fasten them to the brace ends with 3" screws.

22 Use shims to center and stabilize the doors in the door openings. Install the hinges on the doors per the hinge's mounting instructions, and then install the doors via their hinges to the adjacent side panels. If you need to square up the doors, remove the clamps or temporary 3" screws, and pull the adjacent side panels in or out as needed, then permanently attach them to the upper braces with 3" screws. Trim off any excess of the 2 × 2 protruding beyond the side panels.

23 Install the hasp as directed by the manufacturer, and add a carabiner to secure the doors shut.

28

Strawberry Vault

ONCE YOU HAVE your vegetable garden accounted for, it's time to move on to berries. But instead of just worrying about rabbits and deer, now you have to worry about birds as well. And maybe even small children who are too impatient to wait for a strawberry to fully ripen before they snatch it off the vine. Who can blame them? There's nothing quite as irresistible as a glistening berry just waiting to be picked.

To keep your precious crop protected, this strawberry vault is the way to go. It consists of a two-tiered raised planter surrounded by poultry fabric panels that keep pests away. You can even add a padlock to its latch, but if you need one of those to protect your berries you probably have bigger problems. Also, don't let the name of the vault preclude you from thinking it's only good for growing strawberries—lettuce and herbs would feel right at home under its protection as well.

As with any outdoor building project that will be used to grow food, avoid using pressure-treated lumber and instead opt for the naturally weather-resistant variety.

CUT LIST

A. 1" × 8" × 7 ¼" for sides of smaller, inside planter (2)

B. 1" × 8" × 29 ¾" for front and back of smaller, inside planter (2)

C. 2" × 2" × 5" for spacers (4)

D. 2" × 2" × 15" (4)

E. 2" × 2" × 18" (4)

F. 2" × 2" × 24" (8)

G. 2" × 2" × 45" (4)

H. 2" × 2" × 48" (2)

I. 2" × 8" × 24" for sides of larger, outer planter (2)

J. 2" × 8" × 48" for front and back of larger, outer planter (2)

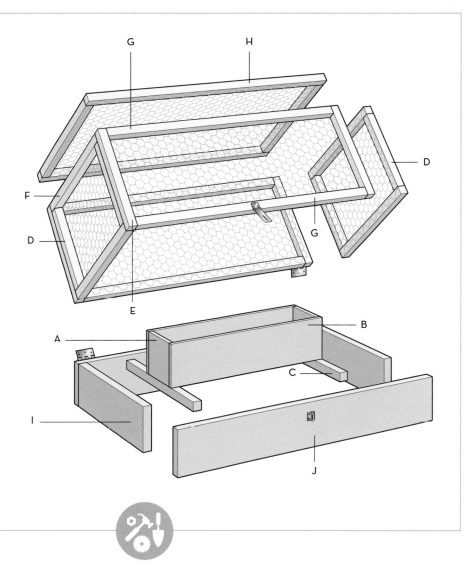

TOOLS & MATERIALS

□ 1 × 8 × 8' lumber (1)
□ 2 × 2 × 8' lumber (7)
□ 2 × 8 × 8' lumber (2)
□ Tape measure
□ Pencil
□ Particle mask, eye protection, hearing protection, work gloves
□ Circular saw, miter saw, or table saw
□ Drill

□ Bar clamps
□ #8 pilot/countersink bit
□ #8 × 2" triple-coated deck screws
□ #10 pilot/countersink bit
□ #9 × 3" triple-coated deck screws
□ 36" × 15' poultry fencing

□ Tinsnips, aviation snips, or wire cutter
□ Stapler
□ ½" staples
□ #8 × 2 ½" triple-coated deck screws (optional)
□ 3" hinges (2)
□ 1 hasp set (consisting of a hinge and a staple)
□ Carabiner (optional)

Making a Strawberry Vault

1. Don safety gear and saw the lumber into the following quantities and lengths:

   - 1 × 8 × 7 ¼" for sides of smaller, inside planter (2)
   - 1 × 8 × 29 ¾" for front and back of smaller, inside planter (2)
   - 2 × 2 × 5" for spacers (4)
   - 2 × 2 × 15" (4)
   - 2 × 2 × 18" (4)
   - 2 × 2 × 24" (8)
   - 2 × 2 × 45" (4)
   - 2 × 2 × 48" (2)
   - 2 × 8 × 24" for sides of larger, outer planter (2)
   - 2 × 8 × 48" for front and back of larger, outer planter (2)

2. For the bottom planter, clamp and attach the two 2 × 8 × 24-inch boards flush to the inside ends of the two 2 × 8 × 48-inch boards with 3" screws. Three screws per end will suffice.

3. For the smaller inside planter, clamp and attach the two 1 × 8 × 7 ¼-inch boards flush to the inside ends of the two 1 × 8 × 29 ¾-inch boards using 2" screws. Again, use three screws per end.

4. Screw two 2 × 2 × 24-inch boards to the bottom of the smaller, inside planter using 3" screws. (Positioning of the planter on these cleats is determined by the desired sun exposure. For example, if you want the vault to open facing south, the upper box should be set toward the back of the cleats—on the north side of the lower box.)

NOTE: *For brevity's sake, when instructions state "attach," the step includes the added suggestion of drilling appropriately sized pilots and countersinks before installing screws..*

5. Now for security. Using 3" screws, attach two 2 × 2 × 18-inch boards to the ends of two 2 × 2 × 45-inch boards. Repeat to construct a second panel. These will fashion the front and back of the vault's cage.

6. Using 3" screws, attach two 2 × 2 × 24-inch boards to the ends of two 2 × 2 × 15-inch boards. Repeat to construct a second panel. These will fashion the sides of the vault's cage.

7. To build the top of the vault's cage, attach two 2 × 2 × 48-inch boards to the ends of two 2 × 2 × 24-inch boards using 3" screws.

8. Staple poultry fence onto one side of each panel you made and on one open side of the larger planter, which will become the bottom of the planter.

9 To join the front and back panels to the side panels, first clamp then attach them together with the optional 2 ½" screws or use 3" screws angled slightly so they don't protrude through the other side. Remember to avoid any adjacent hardware when driving the screws.

10 Clamp the top panel to the ones below and square up the structure. Use a rubber mallet to nudge the parts into place while they're clamped.

11 Attach the top panel to the four panels below using the optional 2 ½" screws or 3" screws angled slightly so they don't protrude through the other side.

12 Position the smaller box inside the larger box so its bottom edge is approximately 1 inch lower than the top edge of the larger planter, using the 2 × 2 × 5-inch boards as spacers. Then, using 3" screws, attach the smaller planter via its cleats from the outside of the larger box through to the ends of the cleats themselves.

13 Set the cage on the planter, then attach the hinges at the back corners of the planter. Use shims to raise the cage slightly when attaching the hinges; this will enable them to function properly.

14 Finally, install the hasp set at the center front with the hasp's hinge on the cage and the hasp's staple on the planter. To secure the hasp, slip on a carabiner.

29

Terraced Herb Garden with Optional Lattice

THIS CORNER TERRACED GARDEN, when coupled with the optional lattice feature, is a welcomed addition to yards that have unused corners or unsightly elements to camouflage, such as air conditioning units and utility boxes. When built in multiples, such terraced gardens can be used to demarcate property lines by punctuating the corners of a yard. Although the garden built for this project was ultimately used as an herb garden, it can also function as a perfect spot for flowers.

If using this garden for herbs or vegetables, make sure to use a lumber with natural weather resistance, but if you plan to grow flowers, pressure-treated lumber is an inexpensive and durable choice.

CUT LIST

A. 2" × 10" × 41" for bottom sides of the planter (2)

B. 2" × 10" × 44" for bottom sides of the planter (2)

C. 2" × 10" × 42 ½" with one end mitered at 45° (1)

D. 2" × 10" × 41" with one end mitered at 45° (1)

E. 2" × 10" × 60 ⅛" for hypotenuse of the upper triangle (1)

F. 2" × 2" × 11 ½" for 3 uprights and 1 as a spacer (4)

G. 2" × 2" × 41" for lattice panel frame (2)

H. 2" × 2" × 42 ½" for lattice panel frame (2)

Lattice

I. 14" × 42 ½" (2)

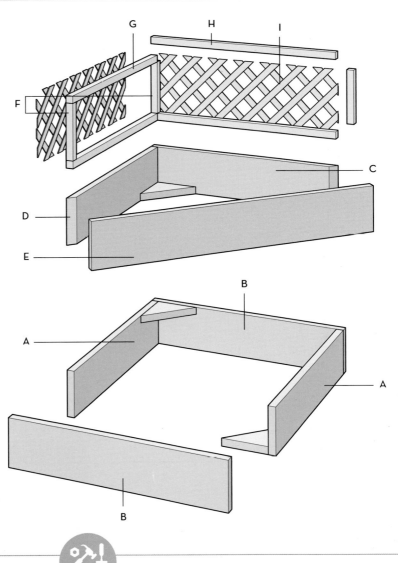

TOOLS & MATERIALS

- ☐ 2 × 10 × 8' lumber (4)
- ☐ 2 × 2 × 8' lumber (3)
- ☐ 2 × 8' lattice
- ☐ Tape measure
- ☐ Pencil
- ☐ Particle mask, eye protection, hearing protection, work gloves

- ☐ Circular saw, miter saw, or table saw
- ☐ Drill
- ☐ #10 pilot/countersink bit
- ☐ #9 × 3" triple-coated deck screws
- ☐ Bar clamps

- ☐ Scrap 2 × 4s
- ☐ #8 pilot/countersink bit
- ☐ #8 × 1 ¼" triple-coated deck screws
- ☐ #8 × 2 ½" triple-coated deck screws (optional)

Making the Corner Terraced Herb Garden

1 Don safety gear and cut the material into the following quantities and lengths:

For the bottom sides of the planter:

- 2 × 10 × 41" (2)
- 2 × 10 × 44" (2)

For the legs of the upper triangle:

- 2 × 10 × 42 ½" with one end mitered at 45 degrees (1)
- 2 × 10 × 41" with one end mitered at 45 degrees (1)

For the hypotenuse of the upper triangle:

- 2 × 10 × 60 ⅛" (1)

For the lattice panels:

- 2 × 2 × 11 ½" (for 3 uprights and 1 as a spacer) (4)
- 2 × 2 × 41" (2)
- 2 × 2 × 42 ½" (2)
- Sheets of lattice measuring 14 × 42 ½" (2)

NOTE: *For brevity's sake, when instructions state "attach," the step includes the added suggestion of drilling appropriately sized pilots and countersinks before installing screws.*

2 To assemble the bottom portion of the planter, attach the 2 × 10 × 41-inch boards flush to the outside edges of the 2 × 10 × 44-inch boards using 3" screws.

3 Now to assemble the triangular, second-tier box. With 3" screws, attach the 2 × 10 × 42 ½-inch board to the end of the 2 × 10 × 41-inch board, creating the two legs of the triangle. To fashion the hypotenuse, attach the 2 × 10 × 60 ⅛-inch board to the mitered corners of the triangle's legs.

4 Cut three right triangles (for cleats) from all the leftover drop pieces of the 2 × 10 boards. Clamp one of the triangles into one top corner of the lower box. Screw the triangular cleat in place with 3" screws.

TIP: *When cutting a board with a miter at one end, it's best to cut the miter first. Then measure from the point of the miter to the straight cut at the other end.*

5 Flip the box over and install a second right triangle cleat on the opposite side of the box and across from the cleat installed in step 4.

6 Install the remaining triangular cleat at the top of the right-angled corner of the upper, triangular planter, using 3" screws.

7. To build the lattice frame, attach two 2 × 2 × 42½-inch boards to two 2 × 2 × 11½-inch boards using 3" screws.

8. Create a second frame by clamping two 2 × 2 × 11½-inch boards to the 2 × 2 × 41-inch boards. With 3" screws, attach them together, but this time only attach one of the 11½-inch lengths to the end of the boards. (The second 2 × 2 × 11½-inch board is used as a spacer only.)

9. Attach the lattice to the back of the first frame with 1¼" screws. On the second frame, attach the lattice on three sides, then remove the spacer.

10. Set the top planter on the bottom planter so that the corners with triangular braces are atop one another. Attach the four-sided framed lattice panel to the top edge of the triangular planter so the lattice side faces out, using 3" screws driven down into the top of the planter.

11. Attach the three-sided framed lattice panel on the adjacent angle of the upper planter, also lattice side out, using 3" screws. Then secure the unframed lattice side to the first frame, using 1¼" screws.

12. Secure together the overlapping upper and lower triangular cleats in the back corner of the planter, using 3" screws.

13. Attach two scrap pieces of 2 × 4 to the inside faces of the upper and lower planter with 3" or optional 2 ½" screws angled slightly so they don't protrude from the other side. The upper and lower planters are now firmly secured together.

Vertical Harvest Pantry

TOOLS & MATERIALS

- ☐ 1 × 3 × 8' pine (4)
- ☐ 1 × 4 × 8' pine (4)
- ☐ 1 × 6 × 10' pine (4)
- ☐ Tape measure
- ☐ Pencil
- ☐ Particle mask, eye protection, hearing protection, work gloves
- ☐ Circular saw, miter saw, or table saw
- ☐ Wood glue
- ☐ Bar clamps (2)
- ☐ Hammer
- ☐ 2" finish nails or box nails
- ☐ Drill
- ☐ #8 pilot/countersink bit
- ☐ #8 × 1 ¼" screws

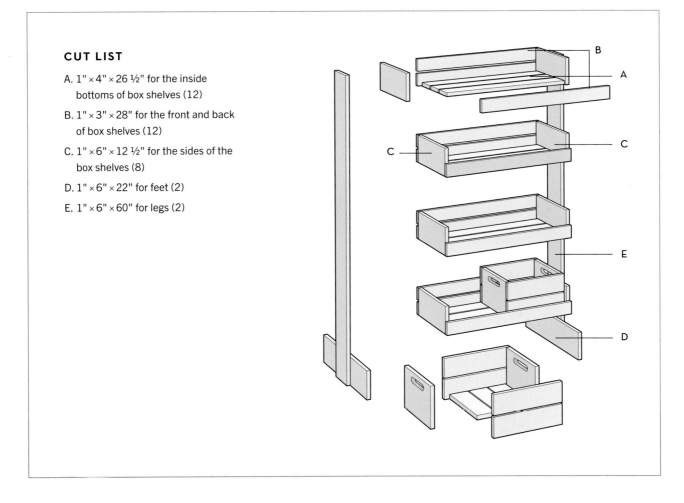

CUT LIST

A. 1" × 4" × 26 ½" for the inside bottoms of box shelves (12)

B. 1" × 3" × 28" for the front and back of box shelves (12)

C. 1" × 6" × 12 ½" for the sides of the box shelves (8)

D. 1" × 6" × 22" for feet (2)

E. 1" × 6" × 60" for legs (2)

BACK IN THE DAY, people made use of root cellars to store root crops. These underground cellars kept produce harvested from the garden cool, dry, and protected from freezing in the wintertime. Nowadays, root cellars have given way to walk-in pantry closets.

The vertical harvest pantry featured here falls somewhere in between the two. It has the rustic, raw quality of days of yore but is perfectly suited to tuck inside a pantry closet or a cool, dark basement corner.

Couple this pantry with the harvest boxes featured on page 56, and you have the perfect spot to store your root vegetables as well as canned goods and canning supplies.

Although this project was assembled using 2" finish nails, it could also be screwed together with 2" screws. If you use screws, it's recommended to use a #8 pilot/countersink bit beforehand to drill pilot holes before driving screws. If you use finish nails, a pneumatic finish nailer will make the job much quicker.

Because this is a project that will be used indoors, it can be built with non-weather-resistant wood. We used ordinary pine, but it could be made with just about any wood, including hardwood for an extra-premium look.

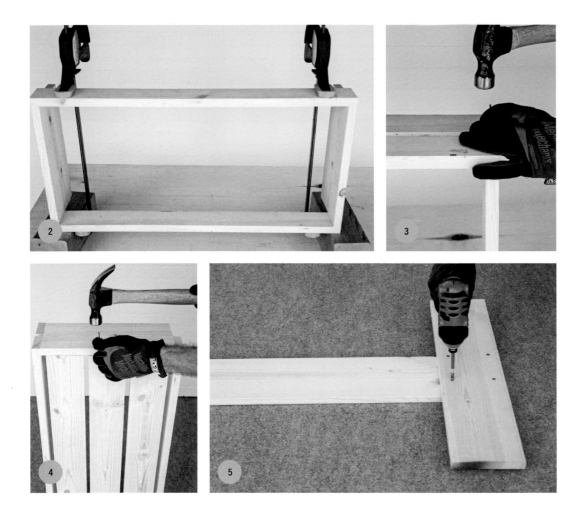

Making a Vertical Harvest Pantry

1. Don safety gear and cut the boards into the following quantities and lengths:
   - 1 × 4 × 26 ½" (inside bottoms of box shelves) (12)
   - 1 × 3 × 28" (front and back of box shelves) (12)
   - 1 × 6 × 12 ½" (sides of the box shelves) (8)
   - 1 × 6 × 22" (feet) (2)
   - 1 × 6 × 60" (legs) (2)

2. Glue, clamp, and nail a front piece and a lower back piece (each 28 inches long) to two side pieces (each 12 ½ inches).

3. Remove the clamps, and attach the upper back to the sides so the edges are flush to complete the box shelf frame. Repeat steps 2 and 3 for the remaining three box shelf frames.

4. Fit three bottom pieces (each 26 ½ inches long) into each box shelf frame, spaced equally apart, and glue and nail them into place.

TIP: *Use a couple of scrap pieces of wood to raise the assembly, thereby creating clearance for the bar clamps.*

5 Center one of the 22-inch-long feet on the bottom of each 60-inch-long leg, then attach them together using 1¼" screws. (Make sure to use a minimum of three screws per foot.) Repeat step 5 to make the lower leg.

6 Lay one leg on the ground and, starting at the top of the leg, position one of the shelf boxes centered front to back and flush with the top. Using 1¼" screws, attach the shelf box into place.

7 Attach the remaining three shelf boxes in the same manner, spacing them 10 inches apart.

8 Flip the entire assembly over and attach the sides of the box shelves to the second leg using 1 ¼" screws.

TIP: *To keep the boxes square and evenly spaced, cut a 10-inch scrap piece of 1 × 6 board to use as a spacer.*

Water Barrel Tower

MY MOTHER AND FATHER, the first gardeners in my life, adhered to the rule that rainwater was better for the garden than "hose water." Most gardeners—and environmentalists—would probably agree. Luckily, if you have a roof and a gutter system, you're more than halfway to a means of collecting rainwater. All you need is a barrel in which to catch it.

Rain barrels can be found in just about every big-box store these days, but for their price tag, they still lack some necessary features. One is good plumbing connections. A second is the fact that they aren't raised. If you plan to attach a garden hose to your rain barrel, raising it is imperative, especially if your garden is more than a few feet away from the barrel. Having a barrel raised even two feet off the ground provides enough necessary pressure to shunt the water from it to a raised garden 10 feet away. It also means we don't have to lug a heavy hose or watering cans from the house to the garden anymore.

CUT LIST

A. 2" × 4" × 23" for the sides of the deck frame (4)

B. 2" × 4" × 26" for the front and back of the deck frames and the top of the lower deck (10)

C. 2" × 4" × 60" for the legs (4)

D. 2" × 4" × 17" for lower deck supports (4)

Lattice

E. 18 ¾" × 43" for sides of water tower (2)

F. for door of water tower, see step #12 in instructions (1)

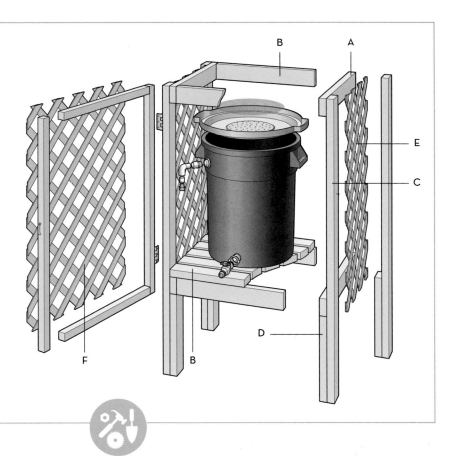

TOOLS & MATERIALS

- ☐ 2 × 4 × 10' pressure-treated lumber (6)
- ☐ Tape measure
- ☐ Pencil
- ☐ Particle mask, eye protection, hearing protection, work gloves
- ☐ Circular saw, miter saw, or table saw
- ☐ #10 pilot/countersink bit
- ☐ #9 × 3" triple-coated deck screws
- ☐ #8 pilot/countersink bit
- ☐ #8 × 1 ¼" triple-coated deck screws
- ☐ Drill
- ☐ 4' × 8' lattice panel, pressure-treated

- ☐ 3" utility hinges (2)
- ☐ 2" zinc hook and eye
- ☐ 32-gallon garbage can with lid
- ☐ ¼" drill bit
- ☐ 1 ½" hole saw or Forstner bit
- ☐ ¾" tank fitting (a.k.a. bulkhead fitting) with Buna-N gasket (2)
- ☐ ¾" male adapter PVC schedule 40 (2)
- ☐ ¾" PVC pipe (1')
- ☐ ¾" female socket PVC schedule 40 ball valve
- ☐ ¾" × ½" spigot x female pipe thread bushing PVC schedule 40 (2)

- ☐ ¾" MH × ½" MIP garden hose adapters (2)
- ☐ ¾" PVC elbow
- ☐ PVC tubing cutter or handsaw
- ☐ Arch-joint-type pliers
- ☐ PVC cleaner/primer
- ☐ PVC solvent cement
- ☐ Pipe thread sealant
- ☐ Window screen
- ☐ Scissors
- ☐ Outdoor caulk
- ☐ Caulk gun
- ☐ 10" mini-bungee cords (2)
- ☐ #8 × 2 ½" triple-coated deck screws (optional)

Making a Water Barrel Tower

....

1. Don safey gear and cut the 2 × 4 lumber into the following quantities and lengths:

   - 2 × 4 × 23" (sides of the deck frame) (4)
   - 2 × 4 × 26" (front and back of the deck frames and the top of the lower deck) (10)
   - 2 × 4 × 60" (legs) (4)
   - 2 × 4 × 17" (lower deck supports) (4)

2. Using 3" screws, attach two 26-inch boards to the ends of two 23-inch boards twice, creating two separate deck frames.

3. Evenly space six 2 × 4 × 26-inch boards on top of one of the decks made in step 2. (The gaps between each board will be approximately 7/8-inch wide.) With 3" screws, attach the boards into place. Two screws per each end of board will suffice.

4. Using the optional 2 1/2" screws or the 3" screws driven in at an angle so they don't protrude from the other side, attach one of the four lower deck supports to one end of each of the 60-inch legs.

5. Working on one side of the tower at a time, use 3" screws to attach two of the 60-inch legs onto the lower deck. The support cleats should be resting directly on the bottom of the lower deck so the supports are supporting the lower deck itself. Flip the assembly over and, again using 3" screws, attach the other two legs into place.

6 With 3" screws, attach the second deck frame into place flush with the top of the 60-inch legs. Flip the assembly over, and repeat on the other side of the tower.

7 Cut two pieces of lattice panel at 18¾ × 43 inches for the sides of the tower. Attach the panels to the sides of the tower with 1¼" screws.

8 To calculate the length of the horizontal rails of the door, use the following formula:

The outside front measurement of the tower minus two material thicknesses equals the width of door rails.

For example, the material thickness of the 2 × 2 used in the water tower pictured here was 1⁵⁄₁₆ inches, so the formula to calculate the width of the door rails was 29½ [the outside measurement of the tower] minus 2⅝" [2 × 1⁵⁄₁₆ inches] equals 26⅝ inches.

9 Cut two 2 × 2 pieces at the length calculated in the last step for the door's rails. Then, cut two 2 × 2 pieces at 43 inches to fashion the door's stiles. With 3" screws, attach the shorter rails to the ends of the longer stiles.

10 Measure the door and cut a piece of lattice to this size. Using 1¼" screws, attach the lattice onto the door frame. If the frame is slightly out of square, you may need to rack it slightly to square it up to the lattice.

11 Attach the door to the tower using the 3" utility hinges installed according to their mounting instructions. Use shims to space the door away from the frame slightly to allow the hinges to function properly.

NOTE: *For brevity's sake, when instructions state "attach," the step includes the added suggestion of drilling appropriately sized pilots and countersinks before installing screws.*

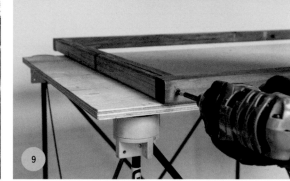

(12) Install the hook and eye at the center of the door and side panel, according to the mounting instructions.

(13) Drill several dozen randomly placed ¼-inch-diameter holes into the lid of the plastic garbage can.

(14) Just above the rounded radius at the bottom of the garbage can, drill a 1½-inch hole with a hole saw or Forstner bit. (Drilling just above the radius will ensure that the water outlet fittings are at their lowest point on the garbage can, while still mounting to a relatively flat surface.

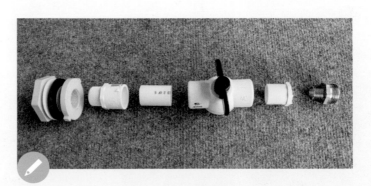

NOTE: *This view shows all the individual fittings you will use to create the water outlet valve assembly in steps 15 through 19.*

15 Apply a bead of silicone around the hole on the outside of the garbage can, then feed one of the tank/bulkhead fittings into the hole from the outside in. Once the fitting is inserted, slip the rubber washer, the flat washer, and then the PVC nut that comes with the fitting from the inside of the garbage can. Tighten with arc joint pliers.

16 Apply pipe thread sealant onto one of the ¾ inch male adapter PVC schedule 40s and screw it into the outside end of the tank/bulkhead fitting just installed. Use arch-joint-type pliers to tighten the fitting, but take care not to overtighten, completing the bulkhead assembly.

17 Cut a piece of ¾-inch PVC pipe at least 1½ inches long, then use PVC primer and solvent cement to glue the pipe into the ¾-inch female socket on a PVC schedule 40 ball valve.

NOTE: *These are the individual fittings that will be used in steps 21 to 23 to create the overflow fitting.*

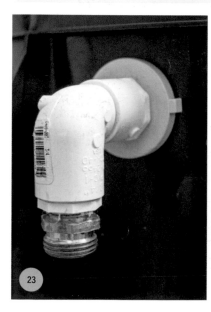

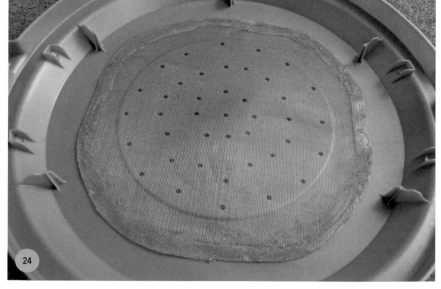

18 Use primer and solvent cement to glue one of the ¾ × ½-inch spigot x female pipe thread bushing PVC schedule 40s into the ball valve. Then, apply thread sealant and thread on one of the ¾-inch MH × ½-inch MIP garden hose adapters, completing the ball valve assembly

19 Use primer and solvent cement to glue the ball valve assembly into the bulkhead assembly.

20 To install the overflow valve, drill a 1½-inch-diameter hole approximately 2½ inches from the top lip of the garbage can.

21 Repeat steps 15 and 16 to mount a bulkhead fitting for the overflow opening.

22 Apply thread sealant to the remaining ¾-inch MH × ½-inch MIP garden hose adapter, then thread it into the remaining ¾ × ½-inch spigot x female pipe thread bushing PVC schedule 40. Finally, prime and glue with solvent cement the previous fitting into the street elbow completing the overflow assembly.

23 Use primer and solvent cement to attach the overflow assembly to the bulkhead assembly.

24 Using scissors, cut a piece of window screen to fit over the holes drilled in the garbage can lid. Use silicone caulk to glue the screen onto the concave side of the lid.

25 Place the lid on top of the garbage can, concave side up, and secure it to the handles of the garbage can with mini-bungee cords.

26 Move the tower structure into position under a downspout, and then tuck your new rain barrel inside.

Mason Jar Bird Feeder

IT'S SAID THAT Henry David Thoreau first wrote of feeding birds as a pastime in the pages of *Walden*. It took another 100 years for the popularity of attracting birds to backyards to begin in earnest. Ever since, armchair ornithologists have been hanging feeders from trees, beams, and shepherd's hooks. We can thank the less-appreciated barnyard variety of fowl—and HVAC parts—for making quick work of turning a Mason jar into a bird feeder.

TOOLS & MATERIALS

- ☐ One 3/16" machine eyebolt and 2 nuts to fit
- ☐ Hacksaw
- ☐ Drill and 1/8" bit
- ☐ One 4" round galvanized steel vent cover
- ☐ Clear silicone caulk
- ☐ 1 quart-size, regular-mouth Mason jar
- ☐ 1 poultry jar feeder, found at farm and garden stores
- ☐ Birdseed
- ☐ #16 single jack electro-galvanized chain, optional

2a

2b

3

4

Making Your Bird Feeder

1. Hacksaw the bolt down to approximately ½".

2. Drill a ⅛" hole at the center of the vent cover; thread a nut onto the eyebolt; slip the eyebolt through the hole, and screw on the second nut.

3. Add a generous—and I mean *generous*—amount of silicone caulk to the bottom of the Mason jar, starting at the edge and working in.

4. Slip the end cap over the bottom of the jar.

5. Grab a tiny bit and drill a dozen or more weep holes into the bottom of the poultry feeder. When the caulk has cured, fill the jar with birdseed and twist the poultry feeder onto the jar. Invert the jar and hang from the eyebolt. To lengthen, add #16 single jack electro-galvanized chain to the eyebolt, if desired.

Mason Jar Butterfly Feeder

IF HONEY BEES and bumblebees are hero pollinators, butterflies are their indispensable sidekicks. These showy lepidopterans gracefully—and hypnotically—flit from flower to flower, adding color to the landscape they help create. Attracting them to our backyards is a gift to us and our gardens. And making their very own feeder—filled with homemade nectar—couldn't be easier.

Making Your Butterfly Feeder

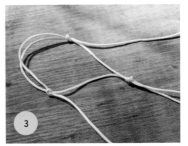

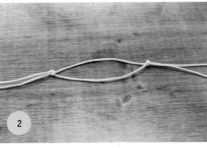

1. Punch or drill a ½-inch or so hole in the Mason jar lid. Cut a bit off the sponge and stuff it into the hole.

2. Cut two pieces of the nylon cord at 34 inches each. Knot both pieces together about 14 inches from one end. Make a second knot 4½ inches from the last knot made. (This will form the opening through which the mouth of the jar will go.)

3. Take one loose strand from each knot and knot them together about 3 inches up from the last knots.

4. Repeat the last step for the other two loose strands. Then, repeat the last two steps one more time. When complete, there should be six knots in all. Slip the Mason jar, bottom up, into the holder just made.

5. Cut off the stem of the silk flower very close to its base. Glue the flower onto the bottom of the Mason jar, taping it firmly down with painter's tape until the glue cures. Finally, knot the ends of the nylon to hang the feeder.

Making The Nectar

Add 4 parts water to 1 part granulated sugar. Boil the mixture at medium-high heat on a stovetop until the sugar is dissolved. When cool, add the nectar to your feeder and hang it in a sunny location.

TOOLS & MATERIALS

- ☐ Drill and ½" (or so) bit or metal punch
- ☐ 1 regular-mouth Mason jar lid and band
- ☐ Small piece of natural sponge
- ☐ Scissors
- ☐ 6' of yellow nylon cord
- ☐ 1 large flat-topped silk flower (red, deep pink, or purple are good choices to attract butterflies)
- ☐ Craft glue, such as E6000
- ☐ Painter's tape
- ☐ Cooking pot and stove
- ☐ Granulated sugar
- ☐ Water

Glass-Bottom Squirrel Feeder

"SQUIRREL!" It's an exclamation that can be heard all across the country. Especially in city parks. So where *did* all those squirrels come from? We can thank our nineteenth-century counterparts for that. Before then, squirrels were primarily a woodland creature. If you saw one in the city, it was most likely someone's pet. Then, in 1847, the city of Philadelphia released three squirrels in Franklin Square—much to the delight of the people who visited it. Towns across the country followed suit, and that's when the squirrel takeover began.

So why feed them? Because watching squirrels munch on peanuts is entertaining.

TOOLS & MATERIALS

- ☐ Piece of 1" × 6" × 4' cedar
- ☐ Table saw or handsaw
- ☐ Jigsaw
- ☐ Drill and bits to fit screws
- ☐ Sander (optional)
- ☐ Paintbrush and outdoor paint (both optional)
- ☐ 1 regular-mouth Mason jar band
- ☐ #6 wood screws
- ☐ #4 flathead screws
- ☐ 1 quart-size, regular-mouth Mason jar
- ☐ Squirrel feed

Making Your Squirrel Feeder

1 Using a table saw or handsaw, cut the board into the following dimensions:

- three pieces at 7" long (sides and front)
- one piece at 10" long (top)
- one piece at 9" long (back)
- one piece at 4" long (bottom)

2 Using the jigsaw, cut a 2-inch round hole in each of the front and side pieces. (The holes should be centered from side to side and their tops should be about 3 inches from the top of the board.) Then, drill two weep holes evenly spaced in the bottom piece.

3 With the table saw or a sander, bevel the back piece's top edge to an 8- to 10-degree angle. Drill and screw the top and back together. Paint the assembly, if desired, with outdoor paint.

4 Drill two holes at all the junction points of the wood pieces. Screw them together with the #6 wood screws.

5 Center the Mason jar band over the front hole of the feeder and screw it into place with the small, #4 flathead screws.

6 Fill the jar with feed—peanuts in the shell seem much appreciated—and fit it onto the band. Attach the feeder onto a post or tree and wait to be entertained.

Jar Seed Starters

IN HIS SEMINAL WORK, *On the Origin of Species*, Charles Darwin accredits James Beekman as the owner of the first greenhouse built in the United States. Constructed in 1764, it was situated on Beekman's Mount Pleasant estate in the countryside of Manhattan Island. Inside the greenhouse, visitors could find unfamiliar tropical specimens such

as orange trees and oleander.

Although impossible to grow such plants to maturity inside a Mason jar, we can certainly start the *seeds* to such plants inside them. Plus, it's a great way to get a jump on the growing season.

Making Your Seed Starters

1. Loosely add geminating mix to peat pots and sow the seeds as recommended on the seed packets. Spray the newly planted seeds with water until saturated.

2. Slip the peat pots into the buckets or pots, and top with an inverted jar. Place the mini greenhouses in a sunny location indoors.

3. A convenient thing about using jars to germinate seeds is they form a perfect enclosure that keeps the seeds and seedlings well hydrated. So well hydrated, in fact, you might not have to spray the seeds with water until you remove the jars.

4. Thin the sprouts according to the recommendations on the seed packets. When mature enough to be on their own, and if the growing season permits, plant the seedlings and their peat pots directly into the ground.

TOOLS & MATERIALS

- ☐ Seed-starting soil, also known as germinating mix
- ☐ 4" peat pots, one for each bucket or pot (these aren't necessary, but they are encouraged, as they make transplanting later much easier)
- ☐ Seeds
- ☐ Plant sprayer
- ☐ Small buckets or pots that measure approximately 4" wide at the top
- ☐ 1 short, wide-mouth Mason jar (a 16-ounce wide-mouth pint jar was used in this project)

Metric Conversions

ENGLISH TO METRIC

TO CONVERT:	TO:	MULTIPLY BY:
Inches	Millimeters	25.4
Inches	Centimeters	2.54
Feet	Meters	0.305
Yards	Meters	0.914
Square inches	Square centimeters	6.45
Square feet	Square meters	0.093
Square yards	Square meters	0.836
Ounces	Milliliters	30.0
Pints (US)	Liters	0.473 (Imp. 0.568)
Quarts (US)	Liters	0.946 (Imp. 1.136)
Gallons (US)	Liters	3.785 (Imp. 4.546)
Ounces	Grams	28.4
Pounds	Kilograms	0.454

TO CONVERT:	TO:	MULTIPLY BY:
Millimeters	Inches	0.039
Centimeters	Inches	0.394
Meters	Feet	3.28
Meters	Yards	1.09
Square centimeters	Square inches	0.155
Square meters	Square feet	10.8
Square meters	Square yards	1.2
Milliliters	Ounces	.033
Liters	Pints (US)	2.114 (Imp. 1.76)
Liters	Quarts (US)	1.057 (Imp. 0.88)
Liters	Gallons (US)	0.264 (Imp. 0.22)
Grams	Ounces	0.035
Kilograms	Pounds	2.2

METRIC PLYWOOD PANELS

Metric plywood panels are commonly available in two sizes: 1,200 mm × 2,400 mm and 1,220 mm × 2,400 mm, which is roughly equivalent to a 4 × 8' sheet. Standard and Select sheathing panels come in standard thicknesses, while Sanded grade panels are available in special thicknesses.

STANDARD SHEATHING GRADE		SANDED GRADE	
7.5 mm	($\frac{5}{16}$")	6 mm	($\frac{4}{17}$")
9.5 mm	($\frac{3}{8}$")	8 mm	($\frac{5}{16}$")
12.5 mm	($\frac{1}{2}$")	11 mm	($\frac{7}{16}$")
15.5 mm	($\frac{5}{8}$")	14 mm	($\frac{9}{16}$")
18.5 mm	($\frac{3}{4}$")	17 mm	($\frac{2}{3}$")
20.5 mm	($\frac{13}{16}$")	19 mm	($\frac{3}{4}$")
22.5 mm	($\frac{7}{8}$")	21 mm	($\frac{13}{16}$")
25.5 mm	(1")	24 mm	($\frac{15}{16}$")

LIQUID MEASUREMENT EQUIVALENTS

1 Pint	= 16 Fluid Ounces	= 2 Cups
1 Quart	= 32 Fluid Ounces	= 2 Pints
1 Gallon	= 128 Fluid Ounces	= 4 Quarts

LUMBER DIMENSIONS

NOMINAL - U.S.	ACTUAL - U.S. (IN INCHES)	METRIC
1 × 2	$\frac{3}{4}$ × 1$\frac{1}{2}$	19 × 38 mm
1 × 3	$\frac{3}{4}$ × 2$\frac{1}{2}$	19 × 64 mm
1 × 4	$\frac{3}{4}$ × 3$\frac{1}{2}$	19 × 89 mm
1 × 5	$\frac{3}{4}$ × 4$\frac{1}{2}$	19 × 114 mm
1 × 6	$\frac{3}{4}$ × 5$\frac{1}{2}$	19 × 140 mm
1 × 7	$\frac{3}{4}$ × 6$\frac{1}{4}$	19 × 159 mm
1 × 8	$\frac{3}{4}$ × 7$\frac{1}{4}$	19 × 184 mm
1 × 10	$\frac{3}{4}$ × 9$\frac{1}{4}$	19 × 235 mm
1 × 12	$\frac{3}{4}$ × 11$\frac{1}{4}$	19 × 286 mm
1$\frac{1}{4}$ × 4	1 × 3$\frac{1}{2}$	25 × 89 mm
1$\frac{1}{4}$ × 6	1 × 5$\frac{1}{2}$	25 × 140 mm
1$\frac{1}{4}$ × 8	1 × 7$\frac{1}{4}$	25 × 184 mm
1$\frac{1}{4}$ × 10	1 × 9$\frac{1}{4}$	25 × 235 mm
1$\frac{1}{4}$ × 12	1 × 11$\frac{1}{4}$	25 × 286 mm
1$\frac{1}{2}$ × 4	1$\frac{1}{4}$ × 3$\frac{1}{2}$	32 × 89 mm
1$\frac{1}{2}$ × 6	1$\frac{1}{4}$ × 5$\frac{1}{2}$	32 × 140 mm
1$\frac{1}{2}$ × 8	1$\frac{1}{4}$ × 7$\frac{1}{4}$	32 × 184 mm
1$\frac{1}{2}$ × 10	1$\frac{1}{4}$ × 9$\frac{1}{4}$	32 × 235 mm
1$\frac{1}{2}$ × 12	1$\frac{1}{4}$ × 11$\frac{1}{4}$	32 × 286 mm
2 × 4	1$\frac{1}{2}$ × 3$\frac{1}{2}$	38 × 89 mm
2 × 6	1$\frac{1}{2}$ × 5$\frac{1}{2}$	38 × 140 mm
2 × 8	1$\frac{1}{2}$ × 7$\frac{1}{4}$	38 × 184 mm
2 × 10	1$\frac{1}{2}$ × 9$\frac{1}{4}$	38 × 235 mm
2 × 12	1$\frac{1}{2}$ × 11$\frac{1}{4}$	38 × 286 mm
3 × 6	2$\frac{1}{2}$ × 5$\frac{1}{2}$	64 × 140 mm
4 × 4	3$\frac{1}{2}$ × 3$\frac{1}{2}$	89 × 89 mm
4 × 6	3$\frac{1}{2}$ × 5$\frac{1}{2}$	89 × 140 mm

COUNTERBORE, SHANK & PILOT HOLE DIAMETERS

SCREW SIZE	COUNTERBORE DIAMETER FOR SCREW HEAD (IN INCHES)	CLEARANCE HOLE FOR SCREW SHANK (IN INCHES)	PILOT HOLE DIAMETER	
			HARD WOOD (IN INCHES)	SOFT WOOD (IN INCHES)
#1	.146 (⁹⁄₆₄)	⁵⁄₆₄	³⁄₆₄	¹⁄₃₂
#2	¼	³⁄₃₂	³⁄₆₄	¹⁄₃₂
#3	¼	⁷⁄₆₄	¹⁄₁₆	³⁄₆₄
#4	¼	⅛	¹⁄₁₆	³⁄₆₄
#5	¼	⅛	⁵⁄₆₄	¹⁄₁₆
#6	⁵⁄₁₆	⁹⁄₆₄	³⁄₃₂	⁵⁄₆₄
#7	⁵⁄₁₆	⁵⁄₃₂	³⁄₃₂	⁵⁄₆₄
#8	⅜	¹¹⁄₆₄	⅛	³⁄₃₂
#9	⅜	¹¹⁄₆₄	⅛	³⁄₃₂
#10	⅜	³⁄₁₆	⅛	⁷⁄₆₄
#11	½	³⁄₁₆	⁵⁄₃₂	⁹⁄₆₄
#12	½	⁷⁄₃₂	⁹⁄₆₄	⅛

NAILS

Nail lengths are identified by numbers from 4 to 60 followed by the letter "d," which stands for "penny." For general framing and repair work, use common or box nails. Common nails are best suited to framing work where strength is important. Box nails are smaller in diameter than common nails, which makes them easier to drive and less likely to split wood. Use box nails for light work and thin materials. Most common and box nails have a cement or vinyl coating that improves their holding power.

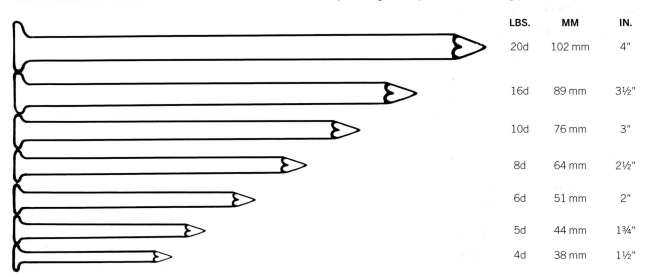

LBS.	MM	IN.
20d	102 mm	4"
16d	89 mm	3½"
10d	76 mm	3"
8d	64 mm	2½"
6d	51 mm	2"
5d	44 mm	1¾"
4d	38 mm	1½"

Index